THE COMMON PATH

to

UNCOMMON
SUCCESS

JOHN LEE DUMAS

THE COMMON PATH

to

UNCOMMON SUCCESS

A Roadmap to Financial
Freedom and Fulfillment

HARPERCOLLINS
LEADERSHIP

AN IMPRINT OF HARPERCOLLINS

Published by HarperCollins Leadership, an imprint of HarperCollins Focus LLC.

Any internet addresses, phone numbers, or company or product information printed in this book are offered as a resource and are not intended in any way to be or to imply an endorsement by HarperCollins Leadership, nor does HarperCollins Leadership vouch for the existence, content, or services of these sites, phone numbers, companies, or products beyond the life of this book.

ISBN 978-1-4002-2110-3 (eBook)
ISBN 978-1-4002-2109-7 (HC)

Library of Congress Control Number: 2020951043

Printed in the United States of America
20 21 22 23 LSC 10 9 8 7 6 5 4 3 2 1

"When you do the common
things in life in an uncommon way,
you will command the attention of the world."

—GEORGE WASHINGTON CARVER

CONTENTS

PROLOGUE

YOU'VE BEEN LIED TO. In fact, we've all been lied to. The reason? Most people don't want you to know one simple fact.

Uncommon success is achievable, and the path is a common one.

This book will reveal a path that will guide you to a life of financial freedom and fulfillment.

How can I be so confident you'll achieve uncommon success? I've walked this path since 2012. After thirty-two years of financial struggle and lack of fulfillment, I found the common path and have never looked back.

You may be asking yourself, "If this path is so common, why don't more people know about it?" The answer is simple. It benefits the "experts" to complicate things, to muddy the waters and add confusion where there should be simplicity.

Why? So they can remain the gatekeepers. So they can remain the one person who holds the "secret key" to success that they alone can unlock for $1,997.97.

We need to make a stand against the gatekeepers. We need to tear down the obstacles they've placed before us. We need to embark upon the common path to uncommon success.

WE LIVE IN a world that provides limitless opportunity and information at our fingertips. With opportunity comes excitement, and with information comes power. This book will show you how to harness your excitement and maximize your power.

Today is the day we take a stand. The common path to uncommon success does not unlock overnight success. It is the north star on your journey toward financial freedom and fulfillment.

Why am I the person to share the wonders of this path with you? For thirty-two years, I listened to the gatekeepers. It wasn't all bad, but I was not on the path to financial freedom and fulfillment.

According to the gatekeepers, I did all the right things: I had a B average during my four years in high school in southern Maine. I attended Providence College on an Army ROTC scholarship. My senior year, the Twin Towers and Pentagon were attacked and my commitment to the Army got very serious very quick. Eight months later, I graduated with a 3.0 GPA and was a part of the first class of commissioned Army officers post 9/11.

After a brief training at Fort Knox, Kentucky, my battalion was deployed to Iraq to serve a thirteen-month tour of duty. It was a rough transition. To go from being a carefree college student to a tank commander leading four tanks and sixteen men in a foreign war was intense. But there I was, twenty-three years old, in Iraq, trying to survive.

As they say, war is hell. Over the course of my thirteen-month deployment, four of my sixteen soldiers gave the ultimate sacrifice.

It was hell.

In their honor, I made a promise to myself. I promised I would never settle for a life that lacked fulfillment. I promised I would never give up in my pursuit of happiness. I promised I would live a life worth living. I owed it to those heroes who died in the line of duty. I would honor their sacrifice by living a life of service, value, and gratitude.

Then, reality set in.

Returning to the "real world" after Iraq was not easy. I suffered from bouts of PTSD (post-traumatic stress disorder) throughout my twenties and struggled to find fulfillment and happiness. I had survived a war, I was financially stable, I had a decent job, but why was I so unhappy and unfulfilled?

Looking back now, the reason is obvious: I was not living the type of life I had pledged to my four fallen soldiers. I was not living a life of service. I was not living a life of value. I was not living a life of gratitude. Instead, I was chasing success, or at least what I defined as success at that time.

I thought success meant money, respect, and maybe even fame.

That warped definition led me to law school, where after one miserable semester, I dropped out. Then I dove into corporate finance, where I suffered in a cubicle for over a year before I simply couldn't take it anymore and handed in my resignation. I then tried real estate, both commercial and residential, thinking that would give me the freedom and fulfillment I desired.

Nope.

This took place over six long and unhappy years. Fortunately, I have always loved learning about how others achieved success. During my six years of struggle, I consumed dozens of business books, online seminars, and, of course, podcasts.

One day I was listening to a business podcast and the host shared a quote that virtually reached out of my earbuds and slapped me in the face.

> Try not to become a person of success,
> but rather a person of value.
> —ALBERT EINSTEIN

I'll share more details of what happened after this *a-ha* moment in chapter 1, but (spoiler alert) I decided in that moment to become a person of value.

Becoming a person of value allowed me to achieve my goal of financial freedom and fulfillment. It's allowed me to finally honor the pledge I made in 2003. It's provided me the opportunity to share how the common path will lead you to uncommon success.

The common path works.

It works because it's simple. It works because it's timeless. It works because of one truth you must never forget.

If you provide the best solution to a real problem, you will find uncommon success.

This book will guide you along the common path until you achieve uncommon success.

Are you ready to get started? Turn the page. The common path to uncommon success awaits.

CHAPTER 1

Identify Your Big Idea

Everything begins with an idea.
—EARL NIGHTINGALE

PRINCIPLE #1: Your common path to uncommon success begins with an idea. A big idea.

There are two mistakes people make when trying to identify their big idea.

MISTAKE #1: They believe their big idea can be something they are *just* passionate about. *I love muffins! I'll open a bakery!*

MISTAKE #2: They believe their big idea is something they *just* have expertise in. *I know how to code; I'll build websites!*

Your big idea is not either/or.

It's not something you are passionate about *or* something you have expertise in. It's both. Your big idea needs to be a combination of your passions and your expertise.

Let's look at scenario one: just passion. Having passion for your big idea is important. You need to be excited to work on your big idea every single day. However, if you just have passion and you're not providing a needed solution to the world, your idea will not gain traction.

Every human is tuned into the same radio station, WIIFM. What's in it for me. Sure, people will be happy you're pursuing a passion, but unless they are going to benefit directly from your passion, they'll never become a customer, you'll never generate revenue, and your big idea will become nothing more than a hobby.

Now let's look at scenario two: just expertise. It's great to be great at something. It's wonderful to share your knowledge with the world. However, if you're lacking passion, excitement, and curiosity for your area of expertise, you will never achieve fulfillment.

The common path to uncommon success is a simple one, but it does take time. If you're lacking passion for your big idea, then one day you'll wake up and realize you're no longer enjoying what you're doing and you'll quit. Also, you'll have competitors who *are* passionate about the area of expertise you've chosen, and they'll win every time.

Now that you can see the flaws in the above two scenarios, let's talk about the final scenario.

This is where you have both passion *and* expertise for your big idea. Your idea truly excites you and provides real value to the world. That is your big idea.

That is your zone of *fire*!

Now it's time to take you through the exercise that will get you to your big idea so you can live every day in your zone of fire.

Sound like a plan?

Your Zone of Fire

For this exercise, you're going to need a piece of paper.

Draw a line down the middle, and on the left-hand side write the word *passion*, and on the right-hand side the word *expertise*.

Set a timer for five minutes and press *start*.

Spend the entire five minutes writing down everything you are passionate about. What excites you? What fires you up? What were you passionate about as a kid, young adult, adult? What would you do tomorrow if you had a completely empty schedule and zero responsibility? Write down everything that comes to mind.

Ding!

Okay, now it's time to move to the right side: your area of expertise. Once again, set a timer for five minutes and press *start*.

Spend the entire five minutes writing down everything you are an expert in. What skills have you acquired? What are you good at? What experience have you gained over the years?

Ask your family and friends how they would respond to the question: What does (your name) do well? You might be shocked at what others consider you an expert in that you thought was "normal."

Ding!

Now it's time to start identifying where your passions merge with your skills—where your curiosity commingles with your expertise.

Start drawing arrows that connect your passions with your expertise. These connections are your zones of fire. This is where you will choose your big idea!

I'll be sharing my story in the next section, but a quick spoiler to give you an example of one of my zones of fire.

On my passion side, I had written down *"having conversations with successful entrepreneurs."*

On my expertise side, I had written down *"facilitating conversations and public speaking from my days in the US Army and corporate finance."*

I realized this was a potential zone of fire and drew an arrow connecting the two.

I asked myself what opportunities existed that would allow me to combine this passion and skill set. That's when the *a-ha* moment came. A podcast!

I loved listening to podcasts that interviewed successful men and women. I had experience conducting interviews in my previous careers. Why not launch my own podcast where I would interview successful entrepreneurs and share their stories with the world?

My big idea had formed and now it was time to act!

My Big Idea

I looked in the mirror.

"Thirty-two years old."

I said those words with a twinge of disgust, even though I had lived a pretty good life. Part of it I've told you about already: Eighteen great years in a small town in Maine with a functional family and plenty of fond memories. Four amazing years at Providence College in Rhode Island as an ROTC cadet and American studies major. Four tough years as an active duty Army officer.

At twenty-six, I transitioned into the Army reserves and took a year off to learn Spanish in Guatemala. I explored the west coast of Costa Rica and prepped for the LSATs (law school entrance exam). I did well enough on the exam that I ended up heading back to Rhode Island to attend Roger Williams Law School and was very excited for the next chapter of my life to begin.

It wasn't immediate, but after a few weeks I knew I had made a grave mistake. Something was off, and I was 100 percent miserable in law school.

It was a strange feeling. I had never been so miserable before, not even during the worst moments in Iraq. Looking back, I realize now I was dealing with PTSD, but at the time I didn't know what was wrong with me. I was unable to focus on anything, which made the endless hours of law school studies torture. I gutted out the rest of the semester, but I knew I wasn't coming back.

I booked a long trip to India and Nepal, had one of the most difficult conversations I've ever had with my parents (and I've had a few), and went off to find my version of eat, pray, love.

India was amazing. It was exactly what I needed: an escape from the "real world."

I enjoyed the noise, the heat, the culture, the food, and the mass of humanity as I explored both India and Nepal, culminating with an epic twelve-day trek way up in the Himalayas, to the base camp of Annapurna, the tenth-highest mountain in the world. But I knew I couldn't hide out in India and Nepal forever, and after four months of zero responsibility I was ready to give my career another go.

For round three, I decided to give the world of corporate finance a try. My thought process was *fast-paced, lots of money, lots of respect.* I landed a job with John Hancock in Boston and the first year was quite enjoyable. I learned a lot, made decent money, and felt like I was on a solid career path.

Then, the 2008 financial crisis struck. I watched people from Bear Stearns and Lehman Brothers walk out the front door with boxes in their hands. My company also had a wave of layoffs, which I survived, but my passion for corporate finance was fading fast. I'll never forget the day when the remaining employees were herded into a large conference room and the CEO proclaimed. "Everyone in this room is here because we want you here, but if you are not 100 percent with us till the end, now is the time to walk out the door."

Those words hit me like an anvil.

I realized in that moment I wasn't even close to 100 percent in and that I owed it to myself and John Hancock to walk out the door.

After that meeting, I walked back to my desk, googled *boilerplate resignation form,* edited a few lines, and printed it out. I signed the dotted line and handed it to my shocked manager, who I'm sure was saying to herself, "Is this kid crazy? Quitting during a time like this?"

I'll speed the story up a little bit to get to the good stuff, my big idea.

My next step was a sales position at a small tech startup company in NYC. I enjoyed living in the Big Apple, but the job turned out to be a bust and after six months I handed in my *boilerplate resignation form* once again.

At this point, I was sick of the living through the cold and long winters of New England and decided what I really wanted was to live in San Diego and sell real estate.

Why? I still don't really know.

However, I was nothing if not an action taker so I jumped in my car, drove cross-country, and settled into a studio apartment in Pacific Beach San Diego, one block from the Pacific Ocean.

I had some success in real estate over the next two years, loved the SoCal lifestyle, and met the love of my life, Kate! (Everything happens for a reason.) With my moderate real estate success in San Diego, a relative back in Maine caught wind and offered me a job.

The job was with the second-largest commercial real estate firm in Maine and came with a five-year partnership track. I had not lived in Maine for more than ten years and the thought of returning home to be close to family was quite appealing. I accepted the job, made the move, and settled into a cozy condo in Portland, mere blocks from my new job.

I really thought I was settling in for the long haul, which is a bold statement for somebody who in the previous five years had left the Army, traveled through Central America, tried law school, fled to India, tested out corporate finance, attempted to make it in NYC, and headed west to San Diego.

I loved my place, I was enjoying reconnecting with family and friends of old, and I believed my career prospects were bright. Then, Maine went into its worst commercial real estate slump in decades.

It was a brutal year.

I remember working so hard on a deal, closing it, then getting a commission check of $316. At the one-year mark, I was having doubts that this was the career for me. Even if commercial real estate had been booming, it was obvious I had very little passion for this industry.

But what else would I do? Was I really going to start from scratch *again?* I was decent at starting from scratch, but at the same time it was exhausting.

I was ready to build something I was proud of. Something I was passionate about. Something I was good at.

That's when I started down the journey that led me to my big idea.

I LOADED UP my iPod Nano with my favorite podcasts and headed out for a stroll. I knew my "career" in commercial real estate was over, but what was next? I was thirty-two years old. Wasn't I supposed to be settled into an amazing career at this point?

What was wrong with me?

As a wallowed in self-pity, my brain focused on the podcast I was listening to. The host was quoting Albert Einstein, and the quote stopped me in my tracks. And now we're back to the *a-ha* moment.

> Try not to become a person of success,
> but rather a person of value.
> —ALBERT EINSTEIN

Wow.

As I shared earlier, it was like someone had reached out of the earbuds and virtually slapped me in the face, and the slap continued to sting as I recalled the error of my ways. Ever since leaving the Army, I'd been chasing my warped definition of success.

I thought becoming a lawyer would give me respect.

I thought corporate finance would make me rich.

I thought real estate would give me freedom and fulfillment.

Wrong, wrong, and wrong again.

Now I understood why. I was spending all my energy trying to become this mythical person of success, but what value was I providing? Upon reflection, the answer was simple: none.

Here was Albert, reaching out from the grave and sharing the winning strategy. Become a person of *value*. I can still see the light bulb that went off in my head that day. In that moment, I committed to become a person of value and let the chips fall where they may.

I didn't know my next step, but I knew chasing success had left me unhappy, unfulfilled, and lacking direction. Providing value could only improve my sorry situation, so why not give it a try?

I continued my aimless stroll, trying to make sense of this revelation. What value could I possibly provide to this world? Then I asked myself one question that changed everything: "What is something I wish existed in the world that doesn't?"

A few thoughts flittered through my mind, but nothing stood out as a great opportunity. Then, I remembered a recent conversation where I was complaining about podcasts:

"I love podcasts that interview successful entrepreneurs and share their journey, but every show only publishes once a week and I'm always running out of content, waiting for the next show to be released. I wish there was a podcast that published an episode every single day. I would listen to that show!"

Light bulb #2!

Why couldn't I create that podcast? Why couldn't I "be the change you wish to see in the world," as shared by Mahatma Gandhi? In that moment, I decided I would be that change. I decided I would become a person of value by publishing a free, valuable, and *daily* podcast interviewing the world's most successful entrepreneurs.

I had no idea where this path would take me, but I was in it to win it. For the first time in my life, I was committed to becoming a person of value and it felt *great.*

My journey has not always been sunshine and rainbows and I've had a lot of bumps along the way, but I've never forgotten the light bulb moment sparked by the words of Albert Einstein. At every fork in the road, I've chosen the path of providing value. I'll be sharing many more details of this journey in the upcoming chapters, but I want to end chapter 1 with a few spoilers.

My first 365 days hosting *Entrepreneurs on Fire* was fun (and tough), but not very profitable. After a full year of hard work, our revenue was just a little over $27,000. However, I never strayed from the path of becoming a person of value. The dollars were not rolling in, but for the first time in my life I was waking up each day with a sense of purpose, excitement, and *fire.* Every day I was focused on providing free, valuable, and consistent content and our audience was growing.

At the thirteen-month mark, something clicked and we had our first $100,000 (net profit) month. We reached a tipping point and we've now had well over a hundred consecutive 100k+ (net profit) months in a row, which we document in our monthly income reports at EOFire.com/income.

These income reports have become the most visited pages on our site, as our audience loves and appreciates the transparency guidance each report provides. We share our financial success in hopes it sparks ideas to be emulated, but just as importantly we show our many failures as warnings of what *not* to do. To add additional value, our accountant and lawyer join us on our income reports so they can share tax and legal tips for entrepreneurs who are in the process of building their business.

We always circle back to the question, "*How can we provide more value to our audience, Fire Nation?*"

Since *Entrepreneurs on Fire* has launched, I've published over 2,500 interviews with the world's most successful entrepreneurs and have generated over eighty-five million total downloads to date. We get over one million listens each month. We've had rock star entrepreneurs you've never heard of, and we've had entrepreneurial legends such as Tony Robbins, Barbara Corcoran, and Gary Vaynerchuk.

Over the years, we've branched out and run the world's largest podcasting community (Podcasters' Paradise). I've published four journals and created countless free courses for our audience, always following the guiding principle of *"How can we add more value?"*

Looking back, *Entrepreneurs on Fire* was a success because it provided the best solution to a real problem. Was *Entrepreneurs on Fire* for everyone? Absolutely not. However, *Entrepreneurs on Fire* filled a void that existed in the marketplace and I've created financial freedom and fulfillment as a result.

The rest of this book will show you how to follow *your* common path to uncommon success. Join us on this road to financial freedom and fulfillment, and prepare to *ignite*!

An Entrepreneur on Fire's Path to Uncommon Success

HAL ELROD ON IDENTIFYING HIS BIG IDEA

Your level of success will seldom exceed your level of personal development, because success is something you attract by the person you become. —JIM ROHN

HAL ELROD was in bad shape, physically, emotionally, and mentally. His life was circling the drain of despair. He looked at himself in the mirror: *How did I get here?*

Hal had enjoyed massive success for most of his professional life. He was a hall-of-fame Cutco sales rep. He left that lucrative position to open his own coaching practice, helping other Cutco sales reps, business owners, and entrepreneurs improve their sales system. Business was thriving.

Until it wasn't.

The 2007 financial crash happened and Hal's business imploded. Hal lost half his clients. He went $52,000 into credit card debt. His house had a foreclosure notice taped to the front door. Hal was stressed, overwhelmed, and unsure of what he should do next. His body fat tripled.

Luckily, a close friend, Jon Berghoff, verbally slapped Hal into reality: *Hal, you've got to start waking up early every morning to exercise while listening to self-help audio. If you want to improve your business, you need to improve yourself.*

Hal wasn't a morning person, but he was desperate. The next morning, he got up and went for a jog. He hated running. Hal hit the play button on a Jim Rohn audio seminar and went back to hating life.

Hal was only half paying attention to the words until a sentence reached out from his earbuds to shake his soul to the very core. *Your level of success will seldom exceed your level of personal development, because success is something you attract by the person you become.*

Hal stopped dead in his tracks.

He was doing zero personal development, and his level of success was a direct reflection of that. Standing at a street corner on a cold morning, Hal vowed to change that part of his life forever. With a renewed sense of purpose, Hal jogged home, rushed over to his computer, and googled *the habits and routines of the world's most successful people.*

Those words led him down a rabbit hole that had him learning from billionaires, world-class athletes, and other top performers. Hal began to realize that he was seeing the same traits and habits repeated over and over again. Success wasn't rocket science. It was a handful of principles that the most successful people in the world did every day.

The first thing that jumped out to Hal was the importance of a morning routine. When he thought about it, of course it made sense. The morning was the perfect time to get into a peak physical, mental, emotional, and spiritual state. The right morning routine would help you learn, grow, and improve every facet of your life. Then, you could take that better version of yourself into your day, which would impact every interaction you had in a positive way. It would improve your motivation, your energy, and your productivity in everything you do.

Hal's next step was identifying the most important personal development habits and combining them into a system. After a lot of trial and error, Hal settled on six practices that were the most important to lasting success. He created an acronym for these six principles, which has since become world famous: SAVERS, for *silence, affirmation, visualization, exercise, reading, scribing* (journaling).

Now that Hal had his system, he got to work. Hal hoped in six to twelve months he would have some success to show for his new daily practice. The reality blew him away.

In two short months, Hal's income doubled, he was in the best shape of his life, and his depression had disappeared. The economy had gotten worse, but Hal's business improved.

Why? Because Hal improved.

Hal told his wife it felt like a miracle. Her response? "It's your miracle morning." In that moment, a movement was born.

Over the next three years, Hal tested, perfected, and improved his miracle morning. On 12/12/2012, he self-published *The Miracle Morning* and sales took off. Since publication, Hal has sold more than 2 million copies, *The Miracle Morning* has been published in 37 foreign countries, and his Miracle Morning Community on Facebook has over 265,000 members.

Hal's mission is to *elevate the consciousness of humanity one morning at a time.*

The movie *The Miracle Morning* was released on 12/12/20, and I'm honored to say that Hal featured my morning routine in this amazing film. I highly recommend checking it out!

On the topic of finding your big idea, Hal had these wise words: "Your big idea may already be a part of your life and you don't even know it yet. It could be one habit or activity you've successfully applied to your life with your own personal spin. I didn't create these principles. They are all timeless and have been practiced for centuries. I simply combined these practices into a system that worked for me. When I realized this system also worked for others, I knew I had to share it with the world."

Hal had a problem. He crafted an amazing solution. The solution turned into his big idea that has now impacted millions of people around the globe.

Thank you, Hal Elrod.

You can learn more about Hal at HalElrod.com.

Check out your free companion course for added support along *The Common Path to Uncommon Success*: EOFire.com/success-course.

CHAPTER 2

Discover Your Niche

PRINCIPLE #2: Identify an underserved niche and fill that void to the best of your ability.

This is an incredibly important step on your path to uncommon success. Unfortunately, it's the step people resist most. Most assume the broader your niche, the more potential customers, clients, and followers you'll have access to.

It makes sense. If you resonate with everyone, you'll be able to carve out a bigger piece of the pie. Of course, you want everyone (and their mother) to buy your product, service, offering. But . . .

When you try to resonate with everyone,
you'll resonate with no one.
—JOHN LEE DUMAS

Please take a minute to think about these words. They will save you months of pain, frustration, and failure.

I could repeat that phrase until I'm blue in the face, but few will listen. They'll reply, "But, John, I don't want to miss out on someone who may give me money!" I understand the point they're trying to make, but if they don't change their mindset, it's only a matter of time before failure and frustration arrive.

Allow me to share a great example of someone who discovered their niche in the nick of time.

Once upon a time, an inventor created an amazing bug spray that killed every bug you could think of. Cockroaches, ants, beetles, termites . . . you get the idea. In big, bold letters on the spray can, he emblazoned the words "Kills every bug in your household." He invested heavily in shelf space at local markets and waited for the money to pour in. Sadly, the waterfall of sales never materialized.

The inventor couldn't understand why his product wasn't selling. It was the best product on the market! In desperation, he hired a person to stand in the bug spray aisle and observe. When someone picked up a bug spray that wasn't his, the employee approached the individual to inquire why.

When the inventor received the results of the project, he was shocked by the simplicity of the findings:

"I have an ant issue, so I'm looking for something that specifically kills ants."

"I have cockroaches; I want something specially designed to kill those buggers."

A light bulb went off and the inventor immediately switched from one broad promise on his product to multiple labels with different promises.

His hundred bottles of "Kills every bug in your household" became twenty-five bottles each of:

"Kills every ant in your household."
"Kills every cockroach in your household."
"Kills every beetle in your household."
"Kills every termite in your household."

Now, he had a specific solution to the exact problem people were seeking. The result? Sales exploded.

His marketing was still 100 percent honest, but now he was successfully following the advice of the great Robert Collier:

> Always enter the conversation already
> taking place in the customer's mind.

Customers were going to the store because they had an *ant problem*, not a bug problem. That was the conversation happening in their mind. When they saw the words "Kills every ant in your household," the conversation loop was closed and the product was purchased. And they all lived happily ever after! (Except for the ants.)

Back to the topic at hand.

This is exactly why entrepreneurs struggle to find traction with their big idea. It's not niche enough. It's not specific enough. You are not entering the conversation that is already taking place in your potential customer's mind. What's the solution?

Step 1. Identify your big idea.
Step 2. Niche down.
Step 3. Niche down again.
Step 4. Keep niching till it hurts.

How do you know when it hurts? It hurts when you become nervous that your target market is too small. That's when you've niched down to a place you can dominate. That's when you've niched down to a place where you can crush your competition, because there is no competition. Now, you can gain traction and serve your customers better than anyone else.

When you reach that point, you've already won.

Remember, within every big idea there's a niche being ignored. Within every big idea, there's a void begging to be filled. It's your job to identify that void and serve those people.

At this point, I usually hear the words, "But, John, how can I create financial freedom in such a small niche?"

Simply put, you might not, and that's fine. The goal of niching down till it hurts and filling a void in the marketplace is to achieve the one thing most entrepreneurs and small business owners never achieve: *proof of concept.*

Once you have proof of concept, you'll gain confidence in your mission. Once you have confidence in your mission, you'll gain traction with an audience. Once you gain traction with an audience, you'll build trust, identify a struggle, and create the best solution.

But we're getting ahead of ourselves.

I want you to picture a boulder at the top of a hill. It's been there for thousands of years.

Our job as entrepreneurs is to push that boulder down the hill. But it's stuck. It doesn't want to move. No matter how hard you push, it doesn't budge an inch. You try everything, but all you get is a strained back and a bulging vein in your forehead.

Then you remember that you're on the common path to uncommon success. Together, we'll discover exactly where to apply pressure to get that boulder to the tipping point. Once we get to the tipping point, gravity takes over and then hang on tight! We are in for one heck of a ride, and what a thrilling ride it will be!

To recap:

1. Identify your big idea.
2. Discover a niche not being served.
3. Niche down till it hurts.

4. Become the best (and potentially only) option.
5. Gain proof of concept, confidence, and traction.
6. Discover where to apply pressure, reach the tipping point, and hang on tight!

Discovering My Niche

The light bulb clicked on.

I was experiencing my *a-ha* moment.

My big idea was to create a podcast that interviewed the most successful and inspiring entrepreneurs in the world. These entrepreneurs would share their failures, *a-ha* moments, and best strategies to help my listeners ignite their entrepreneurial journeys.

I leaped in the air and gave my invisible twin a high five. I was ready to sprint home and get started right away. Then I realized the flaw in my plan: I had never produced a podcast before and didn't know the first thing about creating a podcast.

I had a little experience interviewing people and facilitating conversations, but I knew I was not going to be a good podcast host from day one. If my show was going to be a success, I needed an edge. I needed a differentiator. I needed my show to possess something special and unique so I could stand out from the crowd and create buzz. *I needed a niche.*

I started to think about the podcasts that inspired me. What did they have in common? What did I like about them? What didn't I like? What was I missing? I made a list of what I liked.

- The audio quality was good.
- The hosts asked good questions and did not talk too much.
- The guests were successful and inspiring.
- Success and failure stories were the focal point of the interviews.
- Specific business strategies were discussed.

- A new episode was released often.
- The hosts did a good job summarizing the main points the guest had made.
- The hosts asked clarifying questions when the message was unclear.
- The interviews lasted between twenty and thirty minutes and focused on business stories and strategies.

I made a list of what I didn't like.

- Poor audio quality.
- The hosts rambled and interrupted the guest frequently.
- The hosts repeated stories about themselves that listeners had heard many times.
- The guests didn't share specific stories or experiences, just vague ideas of success and motivation.
- The hosts released new episodes rarely and sporadically.
- The hosts never asked clarifying questions or even seemed to acknowledge what the guest had just shared.
- Interviews lasted for forty-five to seventy-five minutes when there was usually less than twenty minutes of actual value.

Now that I had my list of likes and dislikes, I created a new list of what I believed would make a great show.

- I would buy high-end audio equipment and ensure my guest's audio quality was good.
- I would seek out inspiring and successful entrepreneurs to interview.
- I would always remember my guests were the focus of every interview.
- I would make sure my guests were prepared with stories and strategies from their past successes and failures.

- As the host, I would summarize the key lessons and takeaways from these stories.
- I would always ask clarifying questions to make sure my guest's message was clear.
- I would release the podcast often and consistently.
- I would keep each interview between fifteen and twenty-five minutes, packed with value.

Now I stepped back and looked at my creation. My heart began to beat faster as I realized I had something special here. At the same time, I knew something was missing. I could create this exact podcast and still fail.

How? There were podcasts that already checked every one of these blocks. Plus, the podcast hosts had experience, an audience, and momentum.

I did not.

So, how was I going to attain that elusive momentum? How was I going to gain initial traction and proof of concept? *I had to niche down until it hurt.*

I had to find a void that was not being filled in the podcast marketplace. I had to find a niche that I could dominate from day one, not because I was better than the competition, but because of the lack of competition. So, I asked myself, what is missing?

I looked back over my list and tried to identify an opportunity. One sentence jumped off the page. *A new episode was released often.*

Boom. That was it!

I went and studied the release schedule of my favorite podcasts. *Often* in the podcast world was once a week. That meant every time I listened to an episode, I would have to wait six days for the next episode to air. I remembered being frustrated and disappointed at having to wait so long for the next show.

What if I niched down and did *twice* as many shows as these podcasts? Two per week!

Immediately, I knew that was not niche enough.

Three? No, it wasn't hurting yet.

Seven days a week? *Ouch*. That hurt. It hurt because I knew the amount of work a daily show would entail, but also because I wondered if other people would listen to a daily show.

After a quick search, I found there were *zero* other shows publishing seven days a week in the business space. It dawned on me that the day I released this show, it would be the *best* daily podcast that interviewed the world's most inspiring entrepreneurs. It would also be the worst. It would be the *only*.

Now that was exciting!

Something else dawned on me. If my podcast was going to be good, I had to be good. How was I going to become good doing something once per week? A mere fifty-two times per year? I was going to become a good podcast host by putting in the reps.

Rinse, wash, repeat.

A daily show meant I would be putting in the reps *daily*. Seven interviews a week, thirty every month, three hundred sixty-five per year!

Plus, I would be networking at an incredible rate. Getting the chance to speak to thirty successful entrepreneurs every month was a dream. Building relationships and possibly friendships with these rock stars would be priceless.

Game on.

Lastly, I realized that the higher the barrier, the lower the competition. A daily podcast interviewing the world's most successful entrepreneurs was such a high barrier to entry that my competition would be nonexistent. That was a race I could win!

Now, I was ready to rock. I knew the podcast I wished existed in the world. I looked in the mirror and made the following pledge: *I am going to create the first daily podcast interviewing the world's most inspiring entrepreneurs.*

I was ready for my next step on the common path to uncommon success.

SELENA SOO ON DISCOVERING HER NICHE

Choose the niche that you enjoy, where you can excel and stand a chance of becoming an acknowledged leader.
—RICHARD KOCH

SELENA SOO was experiencing a quarter-life crisis. She was twenty-five, living in NYC with a cute apartment, cuter boyfriend, and what she thought was her dream job working at a women's nonprofit. Despite seeming to have it all, Selena was depressed.

How was this possible? If she couldn't be happy now, would she ever be able to find happiness? It was time for a change, but what?

Desperate, Selena joined a women's life coaching group. During that time, she was introduced to authors and thought leaders who were helping people live their best lives. She remembered thinking, "I want everyone in the world to know about these people."

Selena realized that when people are looking for real transformation—whether it's finding their purpose, starting that dream business, or healing their health or relationships—people aren't just looking for more information, they're looking for inspiration. She wanted to help more people transform their lives by learning from these incredible role models.

Selena was a natural marketing strategist, brand-builder, and superconnector. By combining all three superpowers, Selena carved out a niche in the marketplace that was not being served. Then, she went to work.

Selena *loved* connecting the dots. When she could bring two people together and create an opportunity out of thin air, her soul was set on fire. To gain initial traction and get proof of concept, Selena served her first clients for free.

The strategy worked. Before she knew it, Selena's clients were providing glowing testimonials and referring her to others in need of her services.

Selena's depression melted away as she awoke every day with a renewed sense of purpose. She was helping to spread the stories of inspiring people and giving hope to those who needed it most. Selena went all in on her niche and has since built a seven-figure business that helps experts, coaches, and authors become respected leaders in their industries.

Selena's advice on discovering your niche: *What is the thing you love to do so much you would do it for free?* Once you've identified that, get out in the marketplace and prove your value. Get people massive results for free. Turn them into raving fans, evangelists, and referral-generating machines.

Personally, I love how Selena combined three superpowers into one unique and underserved niche. Alone, each superpower was in a crowded market with a ton of competition. However, by combining her skills as a market strategist, brand-builder, and superconnector into one core offering, Selena became the acknowledged leader in her niche. The rest is history, or in this case, *her*-story.

Thank you, Selena Soo.

You can learn more about Selena at SelenaSoo.com.

Check out your free companion course for added support along *The Common Path to Uncommon Success*: EOFire.com/success-course.

CHAPTER 3

Create Your Avatar

Everyone is not your customer.
—SETH GODIN

PRINCIPLE #3: Your avatar is the north star to guide you along your journey.

Y ou've identified your big idea. You've discovered your niche. Now you're ready for your next step along this common path to uncommon success: creating your avatar.

What is an avatar? An avatar is one single individual. Your avatar is your perfect customer, your model client, the ideal consumer of your content, your products, your services, and your offers.

This is an incredibly important step on the common path to uncommon success, yet it's one of the most ignored. When you know your avatar with absolute clarity, you can operate your business with confidence and speed.

Allow me to explain.

As Seth Godin shared in the quote above, everyone is not your customer. Yet when you ask most entrepreneurs who their avatar is, their reply will be some form of *everyone*. And they'll fail.

Everyone is not your customer. In fact, *most* people are not your customer. There are billions of people in this world. Ninety-nine percent of humans will never know you exist, let alone consume your content and be impacted by your message.

And that's okay.

In fact, that's great. You don't need billions of customers. Podcasters' Paradise, my elite podcasting community, is one of the most successful online communities of any kind in the world and we've had six thousand people join in over eight years! That's less than a thousand people a year, and yet we've generated over $5 million in revenue *just* from Podcasters' Paradise.

How? We know our avatar inside and out. Everything we do in the podcasting space is crafted for our ideal customer. It's our only focus, and as a result, Podcasters' Paradise continues to thrive year after year.

So, how can you craft your avatar? Sit down with pen in hand, and answer the below questions. Remember, you are creating *one* perfect consumer of your content. One single person.

1. What is the age of your avatar?
2. Male or female?
3. Married?
4. Kids?
5. Job? If yes, what?
6. Do they commute to work? If yes, how long?
7. Do they like their job?
8. What are their passions?
9. What are their hobbies?
10. What do they do in their free time?
11. What are their dislikes?
12. What are the skills they've acquired over the years?
13. What value can they bring to the world?
14. What are their life goals, ambitions, hopes, and dreams?
15. What does a perfect day in their life look like?
16. What type of content do they consume? How often?

17. What is their biggest struggle in life right now?
18. What is the solution they are looking for?

After you've answered the above questions, it's time to write out a five-hundred-word bio of your avatar. Use your imagination here and have some fun.

By the time you are done, you should have an incredibly clear understanding of who your avatar is. You should know this person better than some of your close friends.

Okay! You've created your avatar—congratulations! You just completed a critical step in your path to uncommon success that will be your north star for the remainder of your journey.

As entrepreneurs, we'll be faced with thousands of decisions. Every decision is a fork in the road. Should I go left or should I go right? Those who haven't created their avatar spend time, energy, mental bandwidth, and money trying to make these decisions. The worst part? They often choose the wrong path.

Why? Because the only right choice is what is best for their avatar.

Allow your perfect customer to be your guide at every fork in the road.

From this moment on, every step you take on your path toward uncommon success is with your avatar by your side. Without your avatar, you're stumbling in the dark.

The Creation of My Avatar, Jimmy

It was July of 2012. I was in the pre-launch phase with *Entrepreneurs on Fire* and things were progressing slower than I had hoped. I was agonizing over every single decision. Not only was it taking a lot of time, but it was taking a ton of mental bandwidth and was exhausting.

On one of my coaching calls with Cliff Ravenscraft, I complained about how mentally draining every decision was. His response changed everything: *What would your perfect listener want?*

I stumbled and stuttered for a bit, but it was clear I had no clue what my perfect listener would want, because I had not yet created my perfect listener. Then a light bulb went on in my teeny-weeny brain: if I knew who my one perfect listener was, then every decision I was currently agonizing over would become simple.

Every time I encountered a fork in the road, I would look to my perfect listener for the answer and choose the path that was best for them! As soon as I got off the call with Cliff, I sat down to craft my avatar—the perfect listener for *Entrepreneurs on Fire*.

Once I put pen to paper, I couldn't stop. I knew exactly who my perfect listener was; I just had to flesh out the details and keep their best interests at the forefront of every decision I made. To this day, I don't know where the name came from, but at the top of the paper I wrote the word *Jimmy*.

Words flew from my pen as my perfect listener formed before my eyes. When I finally came up for air, over eight hundred words were staring back. As I read over these words, I knew my perfect listener had joined me on my entrepreneurial journey and I was never going to agonize over a decision again.

I won't share all eight hundred words, but I will give you the highlights to show you the depth and fullness I gave to my avatar, who has been the north star for *Entrepreneurs on Fire* every day since.

Jimmy is forty years old. He has a wife and two kids, ages three and five. Jimmy drives to work every day by himself. It's a twenty-five-minute commute. When Jimmy gets to work, he grabs a coffee, says hi to a couple friends on his way to his cubicle, and he spends the next eight hours doing a job he does not like. When his workday ends, Jimmy jumps back into his car for a thirty-five-minute commute home. (He gets stuck in a little evening traffic.) When Jimmy arrives home, he plays with his kids for a bit, has dinner with his family, then puts his kids to bed and spends a little time catching up on the day with his wife. Then, Jimmy finds himself alone on his couch having a little Jimmy pity party.

Why does he spend 90 percent of his waking hours doing things he doesn't enjoy doing, commuting to and from work, sitting in a cubicle at a job he doesn't like? Why does he only spend 10 percent of his waking hours doing the things he loves, like spending time with his kids, his wife, his family? Jimmy needs to be listening to *Entrepreneurs on Fire* every day as he drives into work so he can hear my guests share their worst entrepreneurial moment and the lessons they learned from that moment. This way, Jimmy can start to understand that it's okay to fail if we learn from our mistakes. Then, while Jimmy is driving home, he needs to listen to *Entrepreneurs on Fire* so he can hear my guests share their *a-ha* moments so he can start to understand how great ideas are formed and how to turn those ideas into success. Lastly, when Jimmy is lounging on his couch at the end of the day, instead of having a pity party, he needs to listen as my guests drop value bombs during the lightning round, where they share their favorite book, resource, success tactic, and more. By learning from successful and inspiring entrepreneurs, Jimmy will be armed with the knowledge and courage to take his entrepreneurial leap and create a life of financial freedom and fulfillment.

Jimmy is the perfect listener for *Entrepreneurs on Fire*. Every time I come to a fork in the road, I know with speed and confidence the direction to choose. Gone are the days of spending my own time, energy, and mental bandwidth over every single decision. Now I simply ask myself, WWJW? What would Jimmy want? And my perfect listener provides the answer.

How long should the show be? No more than twenty-five minutes because that is the commute time for Jimmy.

How often should the show be released? Daily, because Jimmy drives to work every weekday, to the gym on the weekends, and needs inspiration seven days a week.

What questions should I ask? The questions Jimmy needs the answers to!

Entrepreneurs on Fire is created for anyone who wants to be inspired by successful entrepreneurs, but it's crafted specifically for one person, Jimmy.

Why do people resist getting so specific with their avatar? Because they believe if they create something to resonate with everyone, they will grow their audience faster and achieve greater levels of success. That belief will lead you straight to the dumpster fire of failure. Without your avatar, you won't have your north star. You'll get bogged down in the minutiae of misery and mental burnout.

> If you try to resonate with everyone,
> you will resonate with no one.
> —JOHN LEE DUMAS

As I type these words, *Entrepreneurs on Fire* generates over one million listens every month.

Is every listener a forty-year-old male with a wife and two kids ages three and five? Of course not. I have listeners under the age of ten and over the age of ninety and they get value out of every episode. However, every decision I make is with Jimmy by my side, and that clarity has kept *Entrepreneurs on Fire* on top for well over 2,500 episodes.

Entrepreneurs on Fire has evolved over the years, as has Jimmy. Your avatar will evolve as well, but until you sit down and craft your version of Jimmy, you'll be missing a key ingredient on the common path to uncommon success.

Jimmy, thank you for your guidance all these years. I couldn't have done it without you.

An Entrepreneur on Fire's Path to Uncommon Success

JON MORROW ON CREATING HIS AVATAR

Don't chase people. Be yourself, do your own thing, and work hard. The right people—the ones who really belong in your life—will come to you and stay. —WILL SMITH

JON HAS LEARNED a lot about avatars over the years, mostly through trial and error. When Jon launched his business, he winged the whole concept of the avatar, and "I can't even tell you how much money I've lost as a result." It wasn't until he began conducting formal research and creating products tailored to his ideal avatar that Jon achieved success.

Today, he serves thousands of customers and generates millions of dollars in revenue at SmartBlogger.com. It all began with understanding his three avatars.

1. Someone trying to build passive income by building a niche site, creating courses, and generating affiliate revenue.
2. Someone trying to become an influencer, authority, and acknowledged leader in their niche.
3. Someone trying to make some money from writing.

Jon believes your avatar will define themselves by the actions they are taking and what they are trying to accomplish.

> Your actions speak so loudly, I cannot hear what you are saying. —RALPH WALDO EMERSON

Jon has a problem with the question *"What is your biggest struggle?"* For your audience to properly reply, they must have done something that would cause them to struggle. In Jon's research, 80 percent of any customer segment are aspiring to do something but have yet to take action.

Better questions are:

1. What are you working on right now?
2. What are you doing with your time?
3. What products have you purchased to help you do that?

If they haven't purchased any products, then they are not very serious, and Jon invalidates them as an avatar. Why? Jon has not found it profitable to try and get people to spend their first dollar. He instead directs his focus to people who are actively spending their time and money in pursuit of a goal.

After gathering the answers to the above questions in the form of customer surveys, Jon moves to one-on-one interviews. His team will speak directly to a minimum of ten people in their ideal customer segment. Every conversation is recorded and translated so they can study the results in depth.

Questions they ask during the interview are:

- What does your average day look like?
- Where are you right now in your journey?
- How do you feel about that?
- How does your family feel about that?
- Where are you going?
- Why did you buy that product?
- What were you hoping to get out of it?
- If you were to have a before-and-after photo, what does the after photo look like? Are you sailing the world on a yacht or working at home in your pajamas?

Your goal with this process is to learn as much about your avatar as possible. Who are they paying attention to and buying from that isn't you? You want to divert that attention to your business.

Jon's definition of winning is *capturing more of your avatar's attention and spend on their objective*. Jon has found that his avatar started out just being interested in something and then became more and more sophisticated over time.

Here's an example of Jon's #3 avatar, *someone trying to make some money from writing*: Over time, they've found writing comes more naturally to them than most. They hear about the term *freelance writer*. They begin to wonder if they can make money as a freelance writer. They do a little online research and begin writing for magazines and websites. They learn about content marketing, email marketing, copywriting. They get their first client and become a part-time free-lancer and sometimes a full-time freelancer.

Jon has found that, in the above scenario, the most valuable person is at the end of that journey, but they are also the smallest audience and most difficult to reach. Those at the beginning are a much larger audience and therefore represent the largest potential revenue pool.

In Jon's own words: "Understanding the flow of money, understanding the attention, that is ultimately what avatars are about. The better you get at it, the more money you'll make and the harder you'll be to compete with."

Thank you, Jon Morrow.

You can learn more about Jon at SmartBlogger.com.

Check out your free companion course for added support along *The Common Path to Uncommon Success*: EOFire.com/success-course.

CHAPTER 4

Choose Your Platform

PRINCIPLE #4: Your platform is how you will share your message
with the world.

get it. Life can be challenging. Achieving uncommon success is
hard. But we can *choose our hard.*

It's hard being unsuccessful. It's hard living paycheck to paycheck
and just scraping by. It's hard being stressed about money all the time.
It's hard not being able to support your family, friends, and loved ones.

It's time to choose your hard.

Yes, the common path to uncommon success is difficult. But given
the opportunity, which type of hard will you choose? The good news?
The choice is yours. The better news? You've chosen the common
path to uncommon success.

The next step in your journey is to choose a platform. You have
your big idea, you've niched down, you've created your avatar, and

now it's time to decide which platform will become the main delivery vehicle for your content.

There are three major platforms to choose from: written, audio, and video.

Written

This platform has been around for a long time. Ever since the printing press was invented (around 1440 in the West, earlier in Asia), the written word has been used to share thoughts, opinions, and knowledge. Over the last several hundred years, the newspaper was a major information source. In the 1990s and 2000s, blogging became a popular format where people could share their thoughts, opinions, and knowledge without having to navigate through traditional gatekeepers.

Those who identified their big idea, niched down, and created content for their avatar grew a meaningful audience. Blogs are often hosted on a website, and many have found success using platforms like Medium and Reddit, or utilizing the publishing options available on social media platforms like Facebook, LinkedIn, and Instagram.

Written content has its pros:

- Written content is easily shareable.
- Many people prefer consuming written content over other platforms.
- Writing is less stressful and time-consuming than producing audio or video.
- It is much easier to edit a written piece of content than audio or video.

Written content has its cons:

- A piece written of content is difficult to repurpose into other forms of content.

- Many people don't like reading.
- Written content has a low barrier of entry so everyone can do it, which results in a very saturated platform.

Although writing is not my main platform, I do produce written content for my email newsletter, blog posts, and social media and find it a valuable and complementary addition to my platform.

Audio

I built my media empire on the back of audio content. Podcasts, radio, and audiobooks are the main ways people consume audio content. In 2012, I chose podcasting as my main content platform because I was an avid consumer of podcasts.

I understood the medium. I loved how podcasting was free, on demand, and targeted content. I could choose the specific topic I wanted to hear more about, listen when it was convenient to me, and not pay a dime. How can you not love that?

Plus, I loved how podcasting could be consumed while I was doing other things. Driving, walking my dog, at the gym, doing the dishes, and so on. It turned mundane tasks into opportunities where I could be entertained and increase my knowledge. I started referring to my commute as "automobile university" and no longer dreaded traffic jams. When it came time to choose my platform, I went all in with audio.

Podcasting has its pros:

- People can listen while they are doing other things, which is multitasking at its best.
- It's free.
- It's on demand. You can listen when you want.
- It's targeted. There are hundreds of categories and subcategories of podcasting. You can find a podcast focused on the exact topic you are interested in.
- It's intimate. Humans are drawn to voice.

Podcasting has its cons:

- There are times when people want or need to see a visual representation.
- Some people just don't enjoy listening to audio content.
- It has a medium barrier of entry, which results in a lot of podcasts and a saturated market.

Video

Humans are wired to be visual. We go through life perceiving and re-acting to the world around us. In many ways, video is a perfect platform. It allows you to incorporate both the audio and written platform into your content production. The only negative when it comes to video is it requires your focus, making any form of multitasking difficult.

The positives are numerous. Video allows you to create one piece of content and distribute that content across every available plat-form. Let's say you create a fifteen-minute video on why intermittent fasting can be beneficial. You can take that video and post it to You-Tube and Facebook, IGTV, LinkedIn, and the many other video plat-forms that exist.

Next, you can then cut a one-minute clip from the video and post it to your Instagram feed, Instagram story, Facebook story, Snapchat, and the many other video platforms that exist for shorter videos, with a call to action to go and watch the full video.

You can then separate the audio from the video and create a pod-cast episode. You can also create a transcript from the video and use it to build a written post. This is the ultimate form of repurposing your content across multiple platforms to allow your audience to consume your content in the manner they enjoy most.

As you can see, video has a lot going for it. With video having so much flexibility, you may be wondering why I chose to create an audio-only podcast. I'll share my reasoning in detail later in this chapter.

Video has its pros:

- Humans are visual creatures by nature and love the visual stimulation video can provide.
- It's free (usually).
- It's on demand, meaning your listeners can pause your video and pick it back up where they left off when the time is right for them.
- It's targeted. You can watch videos on the exact topic you are interested in.
- It's easily shareable.
- It has maximum repurpose capabilities.

Video has its cons:

- There is a lot of prep in the creation of high-quality videos: lights, camera, wardrobe, and so on.
- Creating professional videos is pricey.
- Creating professional videos is time-consuming.
- People are unable to constructively multitask while watching videos.
- It has a medium barrier of entry (anyone with a smartphone) so many people are doing it, which results in a saturated platform.

Your Platform

In the previous chapter, you created your avatar. When choosing your platform, you must choose the platform your avatar desires. The common path to uncommon success is a difficult journey, but the path is clear. Choose a platform, commit to it, and produce the best content possible.

You got this!

How *Entrepreneurs on Fire* was born

When it came time to choose the platform I would focus on, the question to ask was obvious: What would Jimmy want? Jimmy wanted to listen as the world's most inspiring entrepreneurs shared their stories. He would consume these stories during his commute, while at the gym, and while walking his dog, Gus.

Watching videos or reading blog posts was not possible during these times. Listening to audio was. There was only one platform to choose: podcasting.

I was an avid podcast listener. I had fallen in love with the medium. I understood the power of voice and understood podcasting's trifecta of awesome: free, on demand, and targeted content.

Free. People always love free, and podcasting is a no-cost way of consuming great content.

On demand. Podcasting gives you the option of listening when the time is right for you.

Targeted. You get to choose which podcast you press *play* on. The power is in your hands.

A daily podcast was a daunting endeavor, but I knew I had to create the solution that Jimmy was looking for. So, I decided to FOCUS: follow one course until success. Podcasting was the platform my avatar needed and I decided to go all in.

An Entrepreneur on Fire's Path to Uncommon Success

LESLIE SAMUEL ON CHOOSING YOUR PLATFORM

Very simply, a platform is the thing you stand on to get heard. It's your stage. But unlike a stage in a theatre, today's platform is not built of wood or concrete or perched on a grassy hill. Today's platform is built of people. Contacts. Connections. Followers.

—MICHAEL HYATT

THE YEAR WAS 2008. Leslie was a high school science and math teacher. He was working long hours and getting paid next to nothing. Leslie had big goals, lofty aspirations, and the tenacity to make it happen, but at his current income level, he would be an old man before he achieved the financial success he desired. It was time to up his game.

Leslie started poking around online, looking for ways to make some additional cash. After learning about affiliate marketing (which I explain more fully in chapter 16), Leslie decided that was the path for him. After learning more about the process in his online research, Leslie found a forum that was focused on affiliate offers and strategies. He spent hours consuming the content and applying the strategies. Then it happened. On January 18, 2008, he refreshed his affiliate balance and a number that was not $0 appeared. In fact, he had made his first $70.

YAY! It actually worked!

It wasn't much, but it was a start and showed Leslie that he could do this. Leslie continued to spend a lot of time in the forums and realized a couple things: One, the same questions were asked repeatedly. Two, he now knew the answers to most of the questions people were asking.

Leslie got to work being a person of value. He spent hours every day answering people's questions and guiding them in the right direction. Then something funny happened. His income started going up. Way up.

People felt such a sense of gratitude and reciprocity that Leslie was providing so much free value that they were seeking out his offers and buying the products and services using his links.

Leslie doubled down on his efforts in the forum. He became a madman, always jumping in to answer questions and providing more and more value as his knowledge and understanding of the affiliate marketing game grew.

Then, Leslie stumbled onto an e-book about blogging. He read the entire e-book in one sitting. A light bulb went off. Here Leslie was, spending so much time every day in the forums, answering the same questions repeatedly. It was working, but as soon as he stopped being so active, his revenue went down. The e-book convinced him a blog was the solution. With a blog, Leslie could craft detailed and high-quality articles that fully answered the questions people were asking every day in the forums.

Now, instead of re-creating the wheel every day, he could direct them to his blog where they could get the best answer to their question, as well as discover the other content Leslie had created. An additional benefit surfaced as soon as Leslie put this plan into action: Google loved his blog and served his articles as top results when people were searching for affiliate marketing information online.

Now, Leslie was getting more traffic with a fraction of the work. Plus, when he stayed offline for a few days to recharge, his income didn't dry up. People kept finding his blog and signing up for his offers.

Leslie added an email newsletter to his blog and began to leverage other platforms such as podcasting, YouTube, and social media to reach an even bigger audience. His call to action for everything was his blog. This is where all his high-quality articles were, full of links to his affiliate products.

Over time, Leslie added courses, consulting, and coaching to his array of services and quickly became the acknowledged leader for how to build a successful blog. In Leslie's own words: "It all starts with creating content on my blog, providing value to my audience, and helping them in their entrepreneurial journey."

Leslie chose his platform and became the acknowledged leader. Now it's time to choose yours.

Thank you, Leslie Samuel.

You can learn more about Leslie at IAmLeslieSamuel.com.

Check out your free companion course for added support along *The Common Path to Uncommon Success*: EOFire.com/success-course.

CHAPTER 5

Find Your Mentor

*A mentor is someone who allows you
to see the hope inside yourself.*
—OPRAH WINFREY

PRINCIPLE #5: Your perfect mentor is currently where you want
to be one year from today.

A mentor is a critical component on your common path to uncommon success. Unfortunately, most people fail to find a perfect mentor. The reason? They're not looking in the right places.

If I asked an average person off the street who their perfect mentor is, I'd hear names like Richard Branson, Mark Cuban, and Barbara Corcoran, among many other high-profile billionaires.

My response would be: *Oh, so you must want to start a record store?* (how Richard Branson made his first million), or *Oh, so you must want to create an audio streaming service of your favorite sports team?* (how Mark Cuban made his first million), or *Oh, so you must want to create a real estate empire in Manhattan?* (how Barbara Corcoran made her first million). As you can imagine, I'm typically met with blank stares.

My point is simple. Your perfect mentor is an individual who is currently where you want to be in one year. No one can be where Richard Branson, Mark Cuban, and Barbara Corcoran are one year from today. That level of success takes time.

In 2012, I wanted to become a successful business podcast host. I sought out and hired a mentor who had been a successful business podcast host for about a year's time (more on this later).

When you use this approach to find a mentor, you'll be learning from someone who has recently completed the journey you're embarking upon. This will ensure their advice is valuable and relevant. They'll know the rabbit holes and bear traps you must avoid. They'll know where you can take shortcuts and which activities are worth skipping over. They'll be able to connect you to the right people in your industry and recommend the events and conferences you should be attending. The right mentor will keep you moving in the right direction while ensuring that your foundation is solid.

So, how does one find a perfect mentor? First, write out exactly where you want to be in one year's time.

- What have you created?
- What does your day-to-day look like?
- Who are you serving?
- How much revenue are you generating each month?
- What types of projects are you currently working on?

Now that you have a clear understanding of where you want to be in one year, it's time to search for your perfect mentor. Your mentor is currently where you want to be in a year's time, so your goal is to create a list of five individuals that meet these criteria.

You have your big idea, you know your niche and your avatar, you've chosen your platform, now go find the people who are crushing it in those areas. Once you have your list, subscribe to the content each mentor is producing—podcasts, vlogs, blogs, newsletters, social media.

Set aside time daily to consume the content each potential mentor is creating on all their channels. Leave comments, share their content with others, send them kind messages. Your job over the next ten days is to get to know each potential mentor and for them to potentially see you engaging with their content. As you consume their content over the course of ten days, let your intuition guide you.

You'll find yourself drawn to one or two of your potential mentors by the content they are creating and distributing. By day ten, you should have a clear list of who your perfect mentors would be in preferential order. All five would likely be good mentors, but you might as well start your quest for the perfect mentor at the top of your list.

Now it's time to reach out to your #1 ranked mentor. You can reach out to them via email, by filling out their contact form, sending them a direct message via social media, or any other method you uncover. This part is not easy, but make a game out of it. Have fun trying to get your message read by your potential mentor.

Here's a sample message.

Hi Stacey!

My name is John and I really admire the success you've achieved. I've been consuming ALL your content over the last few weeks and it really resonates with me. I specifically loved the interview you recently did with Dan. It really opened my eyes to new opportunities!

The reason I'm sending this message to you is this . . .

My goal is to reach the level of success and lifestyle freedom you've achieved and I'm willing to work my booty off to get there.

I noticed you mentor others, and I'm ready to invest my time, energy, and money into your mentorship program if you'll have me.

My goal is to become your greatest success story, and I hope you give me that chance.

I look forward to hearing from you soon so we can begin this journey.

To success and beyond!

—John

Having personally received mentor requests in every way, shape, and form over the years, I can promise you the above message will strike a chord with your perfect mentor. Hopefully, they will be moved by your message and the mentorship can commence! If not, move on to your next candidate until one says the magic word . . . *yes*. Once you've found your perfect mentor, trust their system and follow their guidance.

You got this!

My Mentorship Story

My big idea was to launch a podcast interviewing the world's most successful entrepreneurs. My niche was to do it seven days a week. I had my avatar dialed in and podcasting pinned as the platform of choice. Now what the heck was my next step? To find and hire my perfect mentor! First, I had some questions to answer.

One year from today . . .

- **What have I created?** A daily podcast interviewing the world's most successful entrepreneurs. I will have 365 episodes published, a growing listenership, and multiple revenue streams that support my business and life.
- **What am I doing day-to-day?** My day-to-day will consist of identifying and interviewing guests for my show, interacting with and providing value to my audience, and running my team. I will also be focused on identifying new opportunities to expand and grow *Entrepreneurs on Fire.*
- **Who am I serving?** I am serving those who are searching for content that will help them ignite their entrepreneurial journey. *Entrepreneurs on Fire* will provide the strategies and tactics my listeners need to create a life of financial freedom and fulfillment.
- **How much revenue are you generating each month?** I will be generating between five and eight thousand dollars a month through at least three revenue streams.

- **What projects are you currently working on?** I will be working on a group coaching program that will allow me to share the knowledge I have gained over the past year with those who are just starting out.

Now that I knew where I wanted to be one year from today, I scoured the business category in Apple Podcasts and made a list of the twenty podcasts that appeared to be running the type of business I wanted to be running in a year's time. I went to the websites of each of the podcast hosts, studied their business models, and whittled my list down to five.

For the next week, I conducted in-depth research on each of my five finalists. I listened to their podcasts, followed them on social media, and subscribed to their email newsletters. I made notes of the podcast episodes I particularly enjoyed so I could reference them at a later point. I made sure to like, comment, and share their social media posts. I hit reply to their email newsletters with a thank-you and my biggest takeaway.

All of this was a lot of work, but I knew it was only for a week and it was for an important cause. This research would determine who I would invest my hard-earned money with. This research would determine who I spent my valuable time with. This research would build the foundation for my success.

By day seven, I was ready to list my five potential mentors in preferential order. Top of my list? A successful business podcast host by the name of Jaime Masters.

She had been podcasting for a little over a year and her show was called *The Eventual Millionaire*. There were a lot of reasons she was my number one choice. I loved that her show was just a little over a year old. This meant she was very connected with her early days as a podcaster. I also believed that her advice would be very relevant and timely, given the fact she was still in the beginning stages of her journey. An added benefit was that we both lived in Maine, which I hoped would give us an opportunity to get together in person to work on my business strategy.

I can still remember how nervous I was to contact Jaime. I knew she was my dream mentor, and if she said no, I would be devastated. I pushed through the fear and composed my first email to her.

Hi Jaime!

My name is John and I really admire the success you've achieved. I've been consuming ALL your content over the last few weeks and it really resonates with me. I specifically loved the interview you recently did with MJ Demarco. It really opened my eyes to new opportunities!

The reason I'm sending this message to you is this . . .

You are a year into your podcasting journey and in one year from today I want to be where you are now.

I want the level of success and lifestyle freedom you've achieved and I'm willing to work my booty off to get there.

I noticed you mentor others, and I'm ready to invest my time, energy, and money into your mentorship program if you will have me.

My goal is to one day be your greatest success story, and I hope you give me that chance.

Plus, I'm a Mainer as well, so we both live in the same amazing state!

I hope to hear from you soon so we can begin this journey.

To success and beyond!

—John

PS—Here's a screen shot of the 5-star review I left on your podcast, you are a wonderful podcast host!

Spoiler alert: I have since become Jaime's biggest success story, and reading over this email gives me the chills as it takes me back to the day I wrote those words, clueless about what the future would hold. With plenty of trepidation I hit the *send* button and told myself it would take at least a week for Jaime to have the time to reply.

Patience was not a virtue of mine so I knew the wait would be tough, but I was in this for the long haul and wanted to assemble a dream team to help me achieve my goals and ambitions. That night I fell asleep with a smile on my face. I felt accomplished and hopeful for what was to come.

Sometime around 3:00 a.m., I awoke thirsty. Using my phone as a flashlight, I navigated to the kitchen and poured myself a glass of water. Since I was holding my phone, I decided to check my email. To my shock, there was a reply from Jaime!

Hi John,

Thank you for the note and the kind words.

I recognized your name as you have been commenting on my social media posts and podcast episodes all week. Thank you for that!

I'd love to jump on a call and discuss my mentorship program with you.

I have an opening in June and if we end up being a fit we could start then.

Does 2:00 p.m. EST tomorrow work for you?

Chat soon!

—Jaime

I did a silent fist pump! My week of hard work had really paid off. I had identified my dream mentor, emailed my request, and it looked like we were going to start working together the following week! This was straight *fire*!

I was very grateful for the commitment I had made to subscribe to her podcast and newsletter, and to follow her on social media. My comments, shares, and replies had not gone unnoticed, and that first impression had gone a long way in her quickly agreeing to work with me and avoiding a lengthy screening process. After a great chat the following day, I committed on the spot to a three-month mentorship that would commence June 1.

We planned to meet at a Starbucks to kick off our first session in person. Jaime assigned me some homework to have ready for our first session and I was not going to let her down. The accountability of having a mentor had already begun!

June 1 came quickly, and as I walked into the Starbucks I realized I was nervous. I had been listening to Jaime's podcast for months now and I felt like I knew her, but was very aware she did not know me except for a few email exchanges and a phone call. I ordered my coffee, grabbed a seat, and waited for Jaime's arrival.

Minutes later, Jaime walked in. A professional business podcast host walking into a Starbucks in southern Maine! After a quick hello and the exchange of a few niceties, a thought struck me: Jaime was just a normal person who, a little over a year ago, bought a $70 mic from Amazon, plugged it into her computer, and pressed the *record* button.

Obviously, it was slightly more complicated than that, but it was comforting to see that this person I had been admiring from afar for so long was a down-to-earth, kind, and fun human being. It gave me even more confidence that I could do this. One year ago, Jaime was exactly where I was today: thinking about starting a podcast, but not sure what was to come, and look where she was now!

The sky was the limit, and I was fired up.

Over the next few months, my mentorship with Jaime went exactly as I had envisioned. She provided direction on where my focus should be. She gave me projects to accomplish with strict deadlines. She connected me with graphic designers, web developers, and other independent contractors to help get my brand and website rocking and rolling.

She also insisted that I attend an event in NYC called Blog World. This would be my first event in the entrepreneurial space, and boy was I nervous. However, Jaime introduced me to her friends who were all speakers at the event, and successful entrepreneurs to boot. Even though my podcast had not yet launched, she encouraged these entrepreneurial studs to be guests on my show, and because of the friendship and trust they had with Jaime, they all agreed.

I had met a ton of people who had agreed to be future guests of my show, and many would become friends in the years to come.

Returning home from the conference, I was more invigorated than ever. These were my people! I finally felt like I was in the industry I wanted to be in, building relationships with people I admired with an idea that was going to shake up the podcast space and add massive value to the world.

I still had one major problem.

What was I going to name my podcast? I wanted a name that would evoke the passion I was feeling about the show I was creating. I wanted people to hear the name and instantly know what the show was going to be about.

Once again, my mentor came to the rescue. She asked me what was a nonnegotiable part of the brand. After thinking for a bit, I replied that since I would be interviewing the world's most inspiring entrepreneurs every day, the word *entrepreneurs* had to be in the title.

Jaime told me to let that word bang around my head for a few days and something I saw or heard would spark an idea that could become the name and brand of my podcast. I was skeptical, but agreed to her suggestion.

It happened fast. That very night, I was folding laundry while listening to *SportsCenter*. Stuart Scott was giving the play-by-play of the basketball highlights from the Miami Heat and Boston Celtics game. Being a Celtics fan, I was listening a little closer than normal. Unfortunately, it was not the Celtics' night as LeBron James could not miss. He was in the zone, knocking down every shot he took.

Then, Stuart Scott said something that made me freeze mid-fold: "LeBron James cannot miss, ladies and gentlemen; he's *on fire!*"

That was it.

Being on fire signifies you are crushing it, in the zone, cannot be stopped. That was exactly who I would be interviewing—entrepreneurs who were *on fire*. I visualized my future listeners scrolling through Apple Podcasts and seeing the name *Entrepreneurs on Fire* and knowing this was the show they were looking for. They wanted to learn from entrepreneurs who were on fire so they could one day become an entrepreneur on fire themselves.

Now came the scary part: This name was *too* good. It was too perfect. There must already be another business with this name.

I ran over to my computer and went to Go Daddy. With shaking hands, I typed in the words "EntrepreneursOnFire.com" and hit *enter*.

The sweetest words I have ever seen appeared on my screen: the domain is available!

Success! I had found the name of my podcast, the focus of my brand, and the direction of my future. I was *on fire*!

The next two months went by like a blur. My weekly sessions with Jaime were keeping me on track and I was making progress. Every day, I worked on my website, social media, and podcasting skills. I scheduled, recorded, and edited my first forty podcast episodes.

I set my launch date for August 15, 2012. I had so much to accomplish—my to-do list never seemed to get shorter.

Then it happened: launch day arrived. I woke up August 15 with only one task. Submit *Entrepreneurs on Fire* to Apple Podcasts, the mothership of podcast directories.

Then out of nowhere I became paralyzed with fear. I had been operating under the assumption that the world needed a daily podcast interviewing entrepreneurs. I knew this was a show that I would listen to, but would anyone else? All the doubts and fears I had been suppressing for months began to surface.

What if I'm not good enough?

What if they laughed at my show, my inexperience, my awkward interviewing style?

What if what if what if?

The biggest *what-if* of all? *What if this didn't work?* It was so comfortable living in my pre-launch world. This *might* work! Yes, it might not work, but it might! Pre-launch is a great place. All your hopes and dreams are fully intact. Sure, you can't have true success in pre-launch mode, but you can't fall flat on your face either.

So, I did what most entrepreneurs do. I came up with some lame excuses as to why I had to delay my launch. When I told Jaime, she was surprised, but my lame excuses were believable enough so she gave me some slack. She insisted I wait no longer than two weeks.

In two weeks, I did it again. Fear won and I pled for Jaime to give me just two more weeks.

She consented and I went back to "perfecting my brand." *Perfecting my brand* is another way of saying *wasting my time doing things that really didn't matter.*

Before I knew it, the date was September 15, 2012. Four weeks had passed since I was supposed to launch. I'm embarrassed to even type these words, but I did the unthinkable: I delayed another two weeks.

Luckily, Jaime was on vacation and I thought I got away with it.

Yay! Two more weeks of pre-launch! Two more weeks of pretending to add value to my brand when I was actually cowering behind the fear of failure.

Then, on September 20, my phone rang.

It was Jaime. The conversation went something like this . . .

Hi Jaime! I hope your vacation was great! I've been working hard over here moving my website sidebar from the left side to the right side, but I think I need to move it back to the left side. What do you think?

John, I am going to say this one time and one time only. If you don't stop messing around and launch your podcast today, I am going to fire *you!*

To say my jaw hit the floor was an understatement. Jaime had always mentored me with a firm hand, but this was intense! As scared as I was of launching my podcast, I was even more scared of losing Jaime as a mentor. Her threat was real. She was sick and tired of my lame excuses.

I was also fed up with my lame excuses, but needed someone to kick me into action. I don't remember how the conversation ended, but I do remember this: I launched my podcast on September 20, 2012, and the rest is history.

Thank you, Jaime.

SHAWN STEVENSON ON FINDING YOUR MENTOR

*A mentor is someone who sees more talent and
ability within you than you see in yourself, and helps
bring it out of you.* —BOB PROCTOR

SHAWN LIVED IN a brick-and-mortar world. He was a trainer and nutritionist at a local gym and took delight in helping his clients improve their health and wellness.

One day, he awoke with the realization that he wanted to help more people and change more lives. Shawn knew the way to accomplish this goal was online, but he didn't have a clue where to start. Then, he saw a program being offered by Tony Robbins called *New Money Masters*.

It seemed like the perfect course at the perfect time in his life. Shawn had already received great value from Tony Robbins years before when he read the book *Awaken the Giant Within*. To Shawn, Tony was a proven commodity. He trusted Tony by reputation, respected his authority in the personal development world, and admired the experience he brought to the table.

Shawn devoured Tony's program and learned the importance of becoming a master at your craft. Tony became a master at his craft of personal development by putting in the reps, day after day. Shawn committed to doing the same with nutrition.

Over the next few years, Shawn put in over ten thousand hours becoming a master in nutrition. Now it was time to share his knowledge with the world. Shawn launched a podcast, wrote a book, and shared valuable content daily on social media. His business was beginning to hit the tipping point when his next mentor walked into his gym.

Ken Balk was seventy-seven. He was an incredibly successful entrepreneur. He had made millions over his lifetime, but his body was
breaking down. Shawn assessed Ken and put him on a plan. That plan
proved to be the magical cure Ken was looking for and he became a
Shawn Stevenson fan for life.

Shawn knew he had provided Ken massive value in his area of expertise and needed the favor retuned. Shawn's financial literacy was
low. He was running a moderately successful business, but dotting the
i's and crossing the t's was not Shawn's forte. Ken was more than happy
to oblige.

Before Ken was through, Shawn had the equivalent of a master's
degree in business finance. Ken gave Shawn permission to start small
and grow gradually. He taught Shawn the importance of investing in
relationships, along with setting proper goals and planning your week,
month, and year. It was a true Mr. Miyagi situation, and Shawn made
the most of it.

In Shawn's own words: "I believe in the Goldilocks approach to mentorship. Not too few, not too many, just the right amount. Don't be tied
to just one guru, and have mentors for different areas in your life. Anyone you admire can become your virtual mentor, and when the time is
right, your next mentor will appear."

Who do you admire? Who can become your virtual mentor today?
Take action!

Thank you, Shawn Stevenson.

You can learn more about Shawn at TheModelHealthShow.com.

Check out your free companion course for added
support along *The Common Path to Uncommon Success*:
EOFire.com/success-course.

CHAPTER 6

Join or Create a Mastermind

*You are the average of the five people
you spend the most time with.*
—JIM ROHN

At the end of every *Entrepreneurs on Fire* episode, I share this quote. In all my years as an entrepreneur, I can think of no greater truth. Who are the five people you spend the most time with? You are the average of those people, for better or worse. For most, it's for worse.

If you want to change your life, change your environment. You didn't buy this book because you're 100 percent satisfied with your life. You bought this book because you want to join us on the common path to uncommon success.

The common path is challenging.

I have no doubt that you love your family. I'm sure you have friends you've been close to for years, maybe even decades. Who in your family is upping your average? Keep them close. Which of your friends are upping your average? Keep them close too.

But who in your top five is a Debbie Downer? Who's the Don Doolittle? It's okay if you want to keep them in your life, but if you want uncommon success, they cannot be in your top five. If you want to be the person they whine to about how tough their life is, how unfair their boss is, how tired and depressed they always are, that's fine, but you'll never reach uncommon success.

But you aren't willing to be held back from uncommon success, now, are you? Of course not—it's the name of the gosh dang book!

To achieve uncommon success, you must spend your time working on your big idea with those who inspire and motivate you. So, how do you surround yourself with people who inspire and motivate? You create a mastermind!

The mastermind I'm referring to is what I call a peer-to-peer mastermind. (You'll see a couple of other kinds in the examples that follow, but this is the one you should start with.) It consists of either three or four people. No more, no less. This mastermind will meet for one hour every week and will have a strict attendance policy. If someone cannot commit to making 95 percent of the weekly meetings, they are not the right fit for your mastermind.

Each meeting is kicked off with everyone taking five minutes to share their biggest success of the week and a lesson learned. Next, a timer is set for thirty minutes and one person will be in the "hot seat." The person in the hot seat shares their biggest struggle and their request of the group. The remainder of the thirty minutes is spent with the other members asking clarifying questions and sharing their advice. The hot seat rotates each meeting, ensuring that everyone gets a hot seat session at least once every three to four weeks.

When the thirty-minute timer goes off, there should be ten minutes left to wrap up the mastermind session. During the wrap-up, each member shares one big goal they will accomplish for the following week's meeting.

The above format is simple, effective, and incredibly powerful. When you are part of a mastermind with people you know, like, and trust, the combination of support, accountability, and shared knowledge is fantastic.

When it's just you, procrastination will win. When two or three people whom you respect are holding you accountable every week, your productivity will skyrocket. You won't want to let them down and will accomplish great things as a result.

So, where can you find the two or three people who will make up your mastermind? You should be looking for people who are at a similar place in their journey as you are. They can be a little ahead or a little behind, but the key is finding those who are motivated, positive, and ready to support you on this roller coaster of a ride we call life.

A mastermind will be a key component on your path to uncommon success, so take your selection process very seriously. Once you have found your mastermind, follow the process outlined above and prepare to *ignite*!

My Mastermind Stories

I'm going to share three mastermind stories with you. The first is from the first paid mastermind I ever joined while the second is similar to the mastermind I encouraged you to create at the beginning of this chapter.

Mastermind Story #1

The date was July 15, 2012. I was over a month into my mentorship with Jaime and things were going very well. We were meeting weekly and I was making progress. Still, it felt like something was missing.

I needed to connect with other entrepreneurs who were at similar places in their journey as I was. I needed to bounce ideas off those who had the same doubts, fears, hopes, and aspirations. I needed to be part of a mastermind.

As with so many things in life, when you begin to look for something, it finds you. I was on my daily walk listening to Cliff Ravenscraft's podcast, *The Podcast Answer Man*. He had wonderfully branded himself the leader of the podcasting industry. He deserved every bit of the success and recognition he was experiencing as he was incredibly knowledgeable, generous, and kind when it came to teaching others the trade of podcasting. I admired Cliff and consumed all the content he shared, both free and paid.

During the podcast episode, Cliff was talking about ways to grow your podcast audience. I was enjoying the content, taking mental notes, and excited to get back and apply these principles to my upcoming podcast launch. During the outro of the episode, Cliff shared that he had recently started a podcast mastermind that consisted of ten groups of ten people. Each group would meet weekly with Cliff providing the support and guidance necessary to maximize the success of our podcast.

I was sold, but then Cliff described the real power of masterminds. He shared that although we'd get a lot of benefit from having direct access to him each week, the real benefit would be the combined support and guidance from the other nine members who made up each group. I must admit, my initial driving force to join this mastermind was the direct access to Cliff, but as he described the additional benefit, it was as if a blindfold had been pulled away from my eyes.

Suddenly, I could see the power of the tribe, and it was magnificent.

I cut my walk short and headed back to my house to sign up before the mastermind sold out. Cliff hadn't even mentioned a price, but it didn't matter. I was joining no matter the price point and I knew the benefit would be incredible.

When I arrived home and opened up the sales page, I saw the mastermind was $3,500 for the year. It was a significant amount of money and I was trying to be very frugal with my remaining funds, knowing I wouldn't be generating revenue with *Entrepreneurs on Fire* any time soon. But I didn't hesitate.

This mastermind was what I needed and I knew this was an invest-ment in myself I had to make. Over the next twelve months, my in-stinct was proven right. I never missed a weekly session and I got to know Cliff on a personal level. I also had the benefit of supporting nine other podcasters as they grew their podcasts into thriving busi-nesses. That $3,500 proved to be one of my all-time best investments.

I'll share a quick story that illustrates just how beneficial being a part of Cliff's mastermind was.

It was December of 2012. *Entrepreneurs on Fire* was in its third month of existence and I had published over seventy-five episodes. I had been in Cliff's mastermind for five months and we had developed a great friendship. He cheered me on as *Entrepreneurs on Fire* roared out of the starting gates.

He encouraged me to attend New Media Expo, which would take place in Las Vegas in January of 2013. Cliff was running the podcast track and was very excited about the lineup. I bought my ticket and was ready to go.

In December of 2012, about three weeks before the event, Cliff sent me an email that forever changed the trajectory of my podcast career.

JLD, hope all is well. Our lead speaker on how to launch your podcast has dropped out. Will you speak in his place?

I didn't hesitate.

It would be an honor!

And, just like that, I was headed to Las Vegas, not as an attendee, but as a main stage speaker!

The event was incredible. I rubbed elbows with all the other speak-ers at the speaker-only parties, lounges, and events. Instead of being one of the thousands of attendees, I was one of a handful of speakers. Also, as one of the few speakers on the topic of podcasting, I was elevated to the "influencer" level in the podcast space. I forged strong relationships with other influencers during the event and went home feeling like I had taken a large step in the right direction as the host of *Entrepreneurs on Fire*.

This opportunity led to many speaking opportunities in subsequent years, and helped my launch of Podcasters' Paradise be a success. The opportunity to speak from the stage at New Media Expo would not have happened had I not invested in myself, joined Cliff's mastermind, and proven that I was committed to making *Entrepreneurs on Fire* a true success.

Cliff gave me that chance and I will be forever grateful. Thank you, Cliff.

Mastermind Story #2

The second story I want to share is about a mastermind I formed with two other friends. This is the type of mastermind I described at the beginning of this chapter and one I recommend every person be a part of.

My weekly peer mastermind consisted of Rick Mulready and Greg Hickman. Rick is an authority figure in online marketing. Greg helps agency owners grow their business.

Every week we would meet for an hour and follow the same format. The first fifteen minutes consisted of each of us taking five minutes to share our biggest win of the week and lesson learned. Next, we set a timer for thirty minutes and the person whose turn it was for the hot seat shared their biggest struggle with the other two members asking clarifying questions and sharing their advice. When the timer went off, we spent the final fifteen minutes wrapping up the mastermind by each sharing a goal we would accomplish over the next week.

We did not tolerate skipping meetings and kept in touch to make sure we were on track with our weekly goals. Projects I would have procrastinated on got finished because I was not willing to face my mastermind and admit failure. That special blend of friendly yet serious accountability is key to achieving consistent success. It pushed all of us to greater heights than we would have attained alone.

There is a special power in the right mastermind, and for years Greg and Rick were my mastermind family.

Twice a year we took mastermind trips. These trips brought us closer as friends and gave us something to look forward to. Every trip, we invited one entrepreneur whom we admired and thought would be a great fit.

One of my fondest memories was a trip we took to San Francisco. I reached out to Tim Ferriss, who lived in SF, and invited him to join us during one of our four-hour marathon mastermind sessions.

He said yes, and I decided to keep his response a secret. As we began our four-hour session, our doorbell rang. Everyone (except me) was confused as to who could be wanting access to our Airbnb. I'll never forget the look on their faces when I opened the door and Tim walked in.

Say hi to Tim Ferriss, everyone!

Everyone's jaw hit the floor. Tim's book *The 4-Hour Workweek* had a profound impact on all of us and we all looked up to Tim as an entrepreneurial stud. After a quick recovery, we had a rockin' mastermind session and Tim ended up taking us out for dinner and drinks around town. It was a magical evening and once again shows the power of masterminds!

Mastermind Story #3

The last story about masterminds is the story of Fire Nation Elite.

About eighteen months after the launch of *Entrepreneurs on Fire*, I was looking for another revenue stream to create for our business. I asked my audience what their biggest struggle was. The overwhelming response was their need for more accountability and a sense of community. Being an entrepreneur is not only hard, but lonely too.

That's when I decided to create a hundred-person mastermind called Fire Nation Elite. A hundred is a big number, so I had to make sure I was setting the right expectations.

I sent an email out to my audience and made the announcement on *Entrepreneurs on Fire.* I sent those interested to an application page where they shared some details about themselves, why they wanted to join, and what they hoped to accomplish.

The applications started pouring in and I jumped on the phone with every applicant.

This mastermind was going to be like a family for years to come and I knew we needed the right mix of people to make it work.

After countless hours on the phone, I had my one hundred. Fire Nation Elite was born, and for the next three years, we were a virtual family.

There were live video training sessions each week, daily interactions in our Facebook group, and everyone had reasonable email access to myself and Kate. It was a lot of work, but each original member was paying $100 a month and people who joined after the grand opening were paying $200 monthly, so we were generating over $10,000 a month for the three years we ran Fire Nation Elite.

When we finally closed the doors, there were tearful goodbyes. We had accomplished a lot over the years and knew this was the end of something special. I'll always look back fondly upon Fire Nation Elite. It was a great mastermind and I learned a lot about being a leader.

Fire Nation Elite, I salute you!

An Entrepreneur on Fire's Path to Uncommon Success

JAIME MASTERS ON CREATING A MASTERMIND

The Master Mind principle: Two or more people actively engaged in the pursuit of a definite purpose with a positive mental attitude, constitute an unbeatable force.
—NAPOLEON HILL

THE YEAR WAS 2010. Jaime was living a "less than fulfilling" life in rural Maine. She had a one-year-old and a three-year-old at home, so her days were busy. She wondered to herself, *Is this it?* Then, she stumbled across the same quote by Jim Rohn that I use so much: *You are the average of the five people you spend the most time with.*

Jaime took an honest look at her top five. She even wrote their names down on a scrap of paper. As she gazed at the names, their lives stared back at her.

It was a bit depressing.

They were kindhearted souls but hated their jobs, were unhappy in life, and had no drive or ambition to improve their station in life. Jaime had the drive, but she didn't know exactly where to start. Sure, Jaime had a degree in information technology and had been providing business coaching to clients with seven-figure companies within her mentor's practice for quite a few years. But the online world was massive and overwhelming, and Jaime didn't have any friends with their own online businesses. She joked that trying to figure out all of the ins and outs of online business was like drinking from a firehose.

Jaime took baby steps.

She launched a blog as an experiment and made the commitment to improve the average of the five people she spent the most time with.

Jaime had run masterminds with her mentor before, so she knew how they worked, but she'd never had a personal mastermind. If her goal was to increase the average of the five people she spent the most time with, she knew a good place to start was a mastermind.

Step one was to find high-profile online entrepreneurs who would join her mastermind. Jaime didn't know any high-profile online entrepreneurs, but that wasn't going to stop her. After some due diligence online, Jaime found a personal development forum where people were asking the same questions she had.

Down the internet rabbit hole Jaime went in her search for successful online business owners.

She began cold emailing the successful online business owners she found.

One person Jaime really wanted in her mastermind was Pat Flynn. He was running a successful business through his blog, SmartPassiveIncome.com. Although he wasn't as huge as he is now, Jaime knew, even then, that he would be a great addition.

Pat responded with a polite no.

Jaime was disappointed but didn't let that no slow her down. Soon, she had several impressive entrepreneurs committed to her mastermind, and she gave Pat one final effort, sharing both the bios of the entrepreneurs she had confirmed and the mastermind format she had perfected in her coaching. Pat responded that he loved her tenacity and the organized way she was going about this mastermind, so he was in.

Jaime let out a whoop of joy and doubled down on making this mastermind a great experience for all involved. Jaime wrote out rules and a structure that everyone agreed to. (*Her actual rules and agenda are at the end of this section!*)

One of the most important rules was attendance. If you missed two mastermind sessions in a row (the meetings were weekly), you had to have a chat with Jaime. If your attendance continued to suffer, you would be kicked out of the mastermind.

Over the years, Jaime has had to boot several mastermind members. Why? Commitment is key to masterminds. A mastermind is a place where you can build deep connections and be vulnerable. Fear and doubt are commonplace along the entrepreneurial journey. Most entrepreneurs tackle these emotions on their own and keep their fears bottled up inside. With the right mastermind, you can share your struggles with others who are experiencing similar emotions. Your mastermind becomes your family, rooting you on and holding you accountable.

Back to Jaime's story.

During the first few mastermind sessions, Jaime felt out of place. Yes, she had assembled this mastermind, but her wins were so small compared to the others that she felt embarrassed to share. However, Jaime realized that when you're surrounded by people who are performing at a high level, you can let it scare and depress you or fuel your fire to achieve higher results than you ever thought possible. Successful entrepreneurs use these opportunities as fuel, and Jaime did too.

Jaime has been running this mastermind for ten years now. They try to meet in person at least once a year and have grown so close that it resembles a family. Remember, Jaime was in the middle of nowhere Maine and this mastermind allowed her to connect with incredible entrepreneurs from around the world.

I'd love to share a quick story of how Jaime's mastermind connected us.

During a mastermind session in 2010, Jaime was challenged to interview millionaires. She did not know a single millionaire, but took the challenge and set off on her quest. Leveraging her new connections, Jaime began to connect with millionaires and launched a podcast called *The Eventual Millionaire*.

A year later, I stumbled across this podcast and—after consuming every episode in a few weeks—reached out to Jaime to be my mentor. In Jaime's own words: "It's crazy to look back and see how the small decisions you made have turned into massive business and life wins. That's what a mastermind can do for you. Surround yourself with the right people who will help you make the right decisions that will impact your life in ways you never could have imagined."

Are *you* in a mastermind? If not, it's time to get crackin'!

Thank you, Jaime Masters.

You can learn more about Jaime at EventualMillionaire.com.

JAIME'S RULES

- Meeting times will be determined in advance and each meeting will last for sixty minutes. (A time will be chosen that works for everyone.)
- It is expected that each member is present and on time for the meeting. If someone cannot attend, please post in Slack at least a week in advance to let other members know.
- Set up a hot seat schedule. If you're in the hot seat and need to swap out the dates, please post in the Slack group to find someone to switch with and update the Google doc.
- If you miss more than two consecutive meetings the group will vote on your continued inclusion.
- Everyone will have an opportunity to speak within the framework of the group. It works best if each member participates equally.
- Everyone is here to support each other. Please keep in mind there will be constructive criticism, but there should be no putting down or criticism of other group members. It should be an open and positive experience for all.
- It is important to note, the mastermind is not just for advice, but it becomes a positive place where you can manifest your goals with a group.
- The mastermind is a group effort and not spearheaded by any one member. Each week the host will rotate, as well as the "hot seat" member. The hot seat member will also contribute one great resource or tool they have recently discovered that has been useful in their business or life.

JAIME'S AGENDA

00:00 The host welcomes everyone (the host is the previous week's hot seat member and keeps everyone on track timewise).

00:10 Host asks everyone to share "wins" from the previous week.

00:10-00:50 Hot seat: One member (rotating weekly/biweekly).

1. What is your challenge and how can the mastermind help?
2. What's the end result you want to have from today's hot seat? (This way, the members already understand what the goal is, so if they get off topic, someone can redirect back to the end goal.)
3. Are there any introductions or resources that would benefit this issue?

00:50 Wrap up (chat about any housekeeping, i.e., if someone needs to be out for travel, etc.).

Check out your free companion course for added support along *The Common Path to Uncommon Success:* EOFire.com/success-course.

CHAPTER 7

Design Your Content Production Plan

Content builds relationships.
Relationships are built on trust.
Trust drives revenue.
—ANDREW DAVIS

It's time. It's time for the next step in the common path to uncommon success. You're armed with your big idea. You know the niche you'll dominate and the avatar you're serving. You've chosen your platform. You have your mentor to guide you and your mastermind to support you. Now it's time to design your content production plan.

At this stage, it's tempting to try and do everything.

You have so many ideas. You have so much hope and excitement. You want to take all your ideas and throw them against a wall to see what sticks.

The problem with that strategy? None of them will stick.

Allow me to explain. Picture two scenarios.

SCENARIO 1: You test all your ideas by going one mile wide and one inch deep.

SCENARIO 2: You take all your focus, energy, and bandwidth and go one inch wide and one mile deep with one single idea.

Of the above two scenarios, which one do you think will make a deeper impression on your audience? Do you think you'll ever be able to gain traction and proof of concept by going one inch deep with multiple ideas? Never.

Eventually, your content production plan can include multiple big ideas, but to gain that elusive initial traction, you need to keep your content *focused*. Whenever you hear anyone clamoring to be omnipresent, ignore them. Omnipresence is amazing when the time is right, but for you, that time is not today.

I will share my first content production plan in the next section, and I attribute its singular focus to my success.

Creating financial freedom and fulfillment requires you to create the best solutions to your avatar's biggest problems. In chapter 3, we created the exact person you are going to serve at the highest level. Every decision you make is with your avatar in mind. Designing your content production plan is no different.

Here are the questions we need to answer to design our content production plan.

1. What calendar system will you use to schedule your content production plan?
2. With what frequency will you deliver your content?
3. Which days will your content be delivered?
4. What is the average length of content you will create?
5. How much time will it take you to create each piece of content?
6. How far in advance will you create the content that is going to be published?

7. What days will you set aside each week for content creation?
8. Who is holding you accountable to your content creation plan?
9. What day of the month will you set aside to evaluate your content production plan to adjust as needed?

These questions will ensure that you have a plan to control your content production. Otherwise, your content production will control you. Now, let's break down these nine questions.

1. What calendar system will you use to schedule your content production plan?

I live and die by my calendar. My workday begins with me analyzing my calendar to see what I have on the schedule. My team knows that if it's not on my calendar, it's not going to happen, period. A big mistake a lot of people make with their calendar is leaving a lot of empty space, assuming they will use that time for something productive. That "productive time" rarely happens. You need to block off your calendar for everything you want to accomplish; otherwise someone or something will find its way into your day and disrupt your flow.

Every day for three months, I blocked off the first hour of my day to write at least five hundred words for this book. What was the result? Every day for ninety days, I wrote for an uninterrupted hour and had over fifty thousand words complete well before my deadline. I love looking at my calendar. It gives me a sense of calm that I have created controls around my day that will allow me to produce the right content for my business. One day may have eight *Entrepreneurs on Fire* interviews scheduled. Another day may have fifteen interviews on others' shows. The next day may have absolutely nothing scheduled except time that I have personally blocked off for projects I am working on. When it comes to your calendar, you have two options: either you control your schedule or your schedule controls you. Which is it going to be?

2. With what frequency will you deliver your content?

One theme repeated throughout this book is the need to create free, valuable, and consistent content. This is how you will build trust with your audience. It's important to note that being consistent does not require you to publish daily content. Instead, to establish the frequency you should be delivering your content, you need to ask yourself the question you should be asking during every major decision in your business: What would my avatar want? Your avatar is the ideal consumer of your content, so allow them to guide you on all decisions when it comes to your content production plan. You crafted your avatar, so use that knowledge to decide the frequency with which you will deliver content. Once a month? Once a week? Every Monday, Wednesday, and Friday?

There is no wrong answer. If you're doing what is best for your avatar, you'll be able to adjust and pivot as you gather feedback from those who are consuming your content. Your content production plan, much like your business, is an ever-evolving entity. If you keep your finger on the pulse of your audience by actively engaging them on a consistent basis, you'll know you're serving to the best of your ability.

3. Which days will your content be delivered?

Action trumps perfection. I believe in those words. I've seen many businesses stall out and fail because they were trying to perfect their content, product, service, etc. At some level, everybody is a perfectionist, so if you're saying to yourself, "That's me, I'm a perfectionist," get over yourself. It's a lame excuse that 99 percent of failed entrepreneurs use. Do you want to sound like entrepreneurs who failed? I didn't think so.

When you're creating your content production plan, please remember you're not designing your gravestone. The best part about being an entrepreneur is that we can (and should) be evolving, adjusting, and pivoting on a daily, weekly, and monthly basis. The process of your content creation is simple:

- Create.
- Publish.
- Engage the consumers of the content for feedback.
- Use feedback to adjust and improve.
- Create the next piece of content.
- Repeat.

Now let's move onto which days your content should be delivered. Use this as a guide and then adjust as you and your business evolve.

Once a week: Publish on Monday.

Twice a week: Publish on Monday and Thursday.

Three times a week: Publish on Monday, Wednesday, and Friday.

Four times a week: Publish on Monday, Wednesday, Friday, and Saturday

Five times a week: Publish on Monday, Tuesday, Wednesday, Thursday, and Friday.

Six times a week: Publish on Monday, Tuesday, Wednesday, Thursday, Friday, and Saturday.

I have tested the above and they work best for me. What will work best for you? I have no idea, so stop overthinking it and take *action*. Oh, and I love you.

4. What is the average length of content you will create?

In life and entrepreneurship, nothing is written in stone. We live in a world that is ever evolving, changing, contracting, and expanding.

Even the age-old idiom "the only two certain things in life are death and taxes" is proving false. Entrepreneurs around the world are flocking to low-tax or no-tax oases, while others are making major breakthroughs in anti-aging research and have the potential to live well past a hundred.

What a crazy time we live in.

I shared that dramatic rant to set up my response to a question I get hundreds of times a month: *John, what is the perfect length for my podcast/ email/video/social media post, fill in the blank?* On the common path to uncommon success, my response is always going to be, *What does your avatar want?* This is not an evasive answer. It's the right answer.

I have an honest revelation for everyone reading this book. I'm probably not going to consume your content. Why? I'm not the person you're creating the content for and I probably won't find it interesting or entertaining. Knowing that, why would you want to receive specific guidance from someone who is not your avatar? Simple answer: you don't.

There will be countless people offering their advice along your journey. My recommendation? Unless they are your avatar, ignore 100 percent of their advice. The common path to uncommon success will arm you with a framework that you can apply to your specific journey. Use the framework, and always have the following phrase top of mind:

What would my avatar want?

So, back to the topic at hand—what is the average length of content you will create? You know the answer; say it with me:

What would my avatar want?

The perfect consumer of your content may want three-minute daily snippets, or weekly sixty-minute roundups, or monthly marathon deep dives. Or, better yet, they may want a combination of all the above.

A quote that I refer to often fits nicely here:

> You don't have to see the whole staircase,
> just take the first step.
> —MARTIN LUTHER KING JR.

Take the first step. Create the length of content you know your avatar wants, then hit *publish*. Once your content is out in the world, engage with those consuming this content, analyze the feedback, adjust, and publish.

This is not a science experiment where you need to follow seventeen exact steps or risk having sulfuric acid explode in your face. It's quite the opposite. Make a decision from the best information you have available, publish, engage, analyze feedback, adjust, publish. When you publish real solutions to your avatar's struggles, be confident your content is making the world a better place.

5. How much time will it take you to create each piece of content?

This is a tricky one. At the end of the day, all we have is time. It would be amazing if we had all the time in the world to create the perfect piece of content that changed the world the minute we hit *publish*.

By now, you're aware how I feel about the word *perfect* as we navigate the common path to uncommon success. (Hint. I *hate* it.) My first interview for *Entrepreneurs on Fire* was a thirty-minute conversation followed by a three-hour editing session (shoot me now). I was mentally exhausted and terrified when I finally finished my editing because I knew there was no way I could publish a daily show when each episode was taking so much time and energy.

This is a great example of where necessity trumped perfection. I knew that a daily show was what my avatar needed, so I released perfection, created systems, and found shortcuts that allowed me to consistently whittle those 180 minutes of editing time down to less than ten. That decrease did not happen overnight but over time and it allowed me to stick to my daily commitment and publish two thousand episodes in two thousand days, over more than five years of daily podcast episodes.

I've seen countless entrepreneurs give up after creating one piece of content because they think every piece will be as time-consuming, draining, and terrifying as the first. I'm here to tell you it gets better. *Much* better. Each time you create a piece of content, your brain is laying the groundwork that will make the next time easier and less taxing. After thousands of hours editing podcast episodes, I now feel like Mozart at the piano. I have hotkeys, shortcuts, and systems that would make the 2012 version of JLD shake his head in wonder. Every time I edit a podcast, I get a little bit better, faster, and more efficient.

The same will happen for you in your creation process.

Time yourself during your content creation so you have a baseline and know how much time to block off so you can stick to your production schedule. But know that your efficiency will increase with each iteration, and soon you will be creating the same content in a fraction of the time. The common path to uncommon success is a step-by-step process. There are no secret shortcuts hidden in these pages—which is precisely why you'll feel so amazing once you've achieved financial freedom and fulfillment.

Stay the course!

6. How far in advance will you create the content that is going to be published?

We have a term for this in the industry: *in the can.* It's simple, sweet, and to the point. How ahead of the game are you committing to staying? How many episodes/articles/videos will you have in the can? This is a personal preference.

What is your comfort zone? My comfort zone is having a minimum of six weeks of episodes recorded, edited, and scheduled. This gives me the comfort of knowing that if something crazy happens in my life or business, I will have some buffer time to see me through. There are some niches where creating this type of buffer is not possible, such as current events. For the rest of us, we can get ahead of the game and stay there.

If you're going to keep your promise of publishing consistent content for your audience, getting ahead of the game is a must. Computers crash, the internet fails, natural disasters occur. I'm not trying to scare you, but I've personally experienced all of the above. Despite those disasters, I published daily podcast episodes for two thousand days straight because I was always six weeks ahead.

Decide how far in advance you'll create content that will ensure consistency even if disaster strikes. Once you've made your decision, it will take a few weeks of hard work to build your buffer, but once you have, the hard work is done and now it's just a matter of maintaining this comfort zone moving forward.

As Warren Buffett has been known to say, "It takes twenty years to build a relationship and five minutes to destroy it." You've worked hard to build a relationship with your audience. You've earned their trust; now keep it.

7. What days will you set aside each week for content creation?

When we bump into somebody we haven't seen in a while, a common question is, "What have you been up to?" My least favorite response is unfortunately the most common one: "Oh, I've been *sooooo* busy!" If you were to probe with the question, "Awesome! What accomplishment are you most proud of over the last thirty days?" you'll get a two-second blank stare, then a reply somewhere along the lines of, "Oh, nothing specific. The kids, the work, the pets, the normal, you know?"

No, I don't know. People on the common path to uncommon success don't know. Those who can't share something meaningful they've accomplished in the last thirty days will have the same answer in thirty months and the same answer in thirty years.

A great book to read about this topic is Bronnie Ware's *The Top Five Regrets of the Dying*. This is a book about people who are at the end of their life and are shocked at how little they accomplished in all the years they lived. They're shocked by the realization that they "just got by," going from one meaningless task to another. Sure, they had grandiose plans, but those plans were always for the future, never the present. Now that their future consisted of mere days, the realization dawned upon them that all their goals, dreams, and aspirations were never going to materialize. They were going to die knowing they flittered away their most precious resource, time, and that realization filled them with regret.

Those on the common path to uncommon success do not die with regret. We arrive at the end of our lives knowing we tried, failed, learned, adjusted, tried again, and eventually succeeded in creating a life of financial freedom and fulfillment. Is this a little dramatic for deciding which days you'll set aside each week for content creation? Not in the slightest.

Your friend who gave you a blank stare and a stammered response when you asked what she had accomplished over the last thirty days did not set aside time each week for content creation. You are on the common path to uncommon success. You are going to set aside specific time each week that will be dedicated to the specific tasks that will move your business and life forward.

This is where your calendar becomes your best friend. For over five years, every single Tuesday was completely blocked off in my schedule. Why? Because that was the day I set aside to record and edit eight episodes of *Entrepreneurs on Fire*. Nothing was more important than getting those eight episodes done. It was the only way I could maintain a daily podcast. I'll dive deeper into this part of my content creation in the next section, but I hope you understand the importance of assigning days of the week to specific content creation.

Let's say you want to create an impact in social media. A great plan would be to block off Friday mornings to create content for your social media for the following week. This will allow you to remain timely with your social media posts while not having to dedicate time each day to create your social media content. The content creation plan could look something like this:

Every Friday from 9:00 a.m. to 1:00 p.m. is blocked off to create seven social media posts for the following seven days.

- From 9:00 a.m. to 10:00 a.m. I will create seven tweets, with at least three linking to a relevant article I found on the web.
- From 10:00 a.m. to 11:00 a.m. I will create seven Instagram posts, with at least four being a hundred words or more.
- From 11:00 a.m. to 12:00 p.m. I will create seven Facebook posts, with a minimum of three being video.
- From 12:00 p.m. to 1:00 p.m. I will create seven LinkedIn posts, with at least two being five hundred words or more.

Guess what will happen if you block off your Fridays in such a manner? You'll get twenty-eight quality social media posts done. You'll deliver free, valuable, and consistent content to your audience. They'll begin to know, like, and trust you. Your social media following will grow, as will your reach, impact, and influence.

Simply put, you'll be on the common path to uncommon success.

On the flipside, what happens when people don't establish a content creation plan for their social media? They wake up each day knowing they should post on each of their social media channels. For a few days, maybe even a few weeks, they do it. Then, the weight of having to sit down and create something every day for all four social media channels begins to weigh on them.

Maybe they have a bad day. Maybe they feel sick, tired, or even worn out. Maybe something outside of their control comes up and they have to attend to it. And, just this once, the social media post doesn't go out.

Sadly, this is the first leak in the dam. A few days later something comes up and it becomes easier to just not post today because the world didn't end when they didn't post last time. Then, more situations arise and before they know it, weeks have gone by without meaningful social media content production. The momentum starts to dissipate, the audience growth fades, the leads slow down, and a feeling of helplessness sets in. Another entrepreneur, with the best of intentions, fades away into the sunset.

Again, do I have a flair for the dramatic? Yes. But I have seen a version of the above play out thousands of times. In fact, we have a term for it in podcasting: podfading.

My friends, we are on the common path to uncommon success. We do the little things right, because doing the little things right enough times leads to massive results, and massive results lead to financial freedom and fulfillment.

It's easy to set aside a few hours each week for content creation. It's also easy not to. In this case, choose your easy. Use your calendar wisely and block off time each week for the critical tasks that fuel your business.

There are two more points I want to make before we conclude this section.

The first point is about quality. Would you create better content if you had a block of time set aside each week purely for content creation or if you went into content creation mode each day to publish that day's obligatory social media post? I think you know the answer.

The second point is about efficiency.

Our brain is like a computer in many ways. Our brain has to "turn on" when we want to use it for specific tasks, and it takes a while to warm up. However, once your brain is in the groove, the magic just seems to flow.

I set aside time each day to write this book. It's hard to get my brain in the groove, but after five minutes the words start to flow and I keep my foot on the gas. If you find yourself "booting up your brain" each day just to create one piece of social media content, you're being very inefficient with content creation. On the common path to uncommon success, we don't accept inefficient content creation, as that leads to the dreaded entrepreneurial fade.

Commit to setting time aside each week for specific content creation. By committing to that one task, you're committing to long-term success.

8. Who is holding you accountable to your content creation plan?

Another regret of the dying that Bronnie Ware wrote about is they wished they hadn't let the opinions of others dictate the course of their life. Another way to put it? They surrounded themselves with the wrong people. They valued the opinions of the wrong people. They took advice from the wrong people. As a result, during the last days of their lives, they realized they had taken the wrong path in life.

You are on the common path to uncommon success. It's important to love those who love and support you. I'm sure your mother wishes the best for you. Your dad is likely rooting for your success. But they are clueless as to the direction your life should lead.

Sadly, many times, they are trying to redo their life failures through you. Whenever you hear the words "I sacrificed *everything* for you," it really means, "I failed, and now I'm pushing my hopes and dreams that have wilted and died upon you, because you are my last hope at not completely regretting my life."

Harsh, but true.

If your parents/siblings/loved ones truly understood life, they would encourage you to chase your hopes and dreams, to work hard every day to make a difference in the world, and to create an impact in an area that makes you and those around you happy. Every time I find myself working too hard or too long on things I don't find joy in, I remember the lyrics by Kansas, "All we are is dust in the wind."

Forty thousand years ago, it was important to stick by your tribe through thick and thin. Your tribe provided safety and security as you roamed the sub-Sahara valley. We live in a different world today, and this book is designed to guide you in making the choices that will give you the best opportunity to find happiness and fulfillment in your life.

Chapter 6 was focused on creating or joining a mastermind of people you admire, respect, and enjoy spending time with. These individuals are also on the common path to uncommon success. They've seen the light. They know a life of financial freedom and fulfillment is possible and are committed to attaining uncommon success through hard work, commitment, and being a person of value.

These are the people who will hold you accountable to your content creation plan. These are the people who will make sure you put action before perfectionism. These are the people who will celebrate your successes and help you learn from your failures. Your tribe is out there: find them, embrace them, support them, and they will support you in achieving success beyond your wildest dreams.

You got this!

9. What day of the month will you set aside to evaluate your content production plan to adjust as needed?

In the Army, one of our most valuable trainings was called AARs, After-Action Reviews. The key word is *action*. In the Army, we had a bias toward action, "because a good plan now is better than a great plan later."

Everything on the common path to uncommon success is geared toward action. Without action, there's nothing to get feedback on, nothing to adjust and improve upon, no pivots to be made. Since you've made it this far on the common path to uncommon success, I know you're an action taker.

Now it's time to explain the importance of reflection and evaluation. This is where the gold is. I've always loved the saying *going a million miles an hour in the wrong direction will take you a million miles in the wrong direction*. It's important to move fast and break things, but even more important to identify why things broke.

Every month, you should set aside one day where your team is evaluating the content production plan. You need to identify what is working in this plan. You need to identify what is not. You need to come up with plans to fix the leaks and ignite what's working. You need to make sure you are moving in the right direction.

This day of reflection and evaluation will allow you to keep a finger on the pulse of your business.

We all stray from our north star, but those who become aware quickly and readjust continuously are the ones who remain successful month over month, year over year.

This is one of the main reasons we've been publishing income reports every month since 2013. These income reports are very helpful for our audience because they show both what's working in our business and what's not. They are also incredibly helpful to our team, ensuring we remain accountable for every dollar that comes into our business, as well as what goes out. Every dollar we earn is documented, and every dollar we spend is scrutinized. It's allowed us to keep our profit margins at incredibly high levels because every time we see them slipping, we dive deep into the cause, and if possible, make the necessary adjustments to get back to where we want to be.

I've heard the stories of businesses with multiple small revenue leaks that went unattended for years. Those small leaks add up to massive losses over time and often bankrupt a business that could have otherwise been successful. All that leaking revenue could have been invested in marketing, infrastructure, building out a bigger team, and more, yet instead it went down the drain of false hopes and shattered dreams.

Just one dedicated day a month is all it takes to keep your ship sealed tight and headed in the right direction. You owe it to yourself, your team, and those who gain so much value from the incredible content you share to stay afloat.

You got this!

My Content Production Plan

Now it's time to walk through how I created my content production plan. Before I dive in, it's important to remember that nothing you create on the common path to uncommon success is etched in stone. Everything evolves.

The same goes for your content production plan. It will evolve, it will morph, it will adjust, and it will improve as you continue to create content and identify what works best for you, your business, and your avatar. But we must begin with a foundation; otherwise you'll have nothing to build upon.

Below is my initial foundation.

1. What calendar system will you use to schedule your content production plan?

Before starting my entrepreneurial journey, my calendar was controlled by whomever my boss happened to be at the time. I can remember opening my calendar each day with dread, seeing meeting after endless meeting populating almost every working hour. With the little white space I had on my calendar, I would stare blankly at my computer and drift off to never-never land, before being ripped back into reality and whatever soul-sucking task I had to accomplish next.

When I started my entrepreneurial journey, I remember opening my calendar and seeing nothing *but* white space. I felt lost. I felt anxious. I felt aimless. Where was the person who was supposed to be telling me what to do?

As an officer in the US Army, I had a commanding officer handing down orders daily. Same thing as a real estate broker and as a corporate drone. Now, the only person who was present and able to provide direction was the face reflecting off my blank calendar. Me.

It was time to put my big boy pants on. If this ship was going to leave the dock, I was going to be the one to lift anchor.

I started by googling *best calendar and scheduling tool.* After reading a few articles and viewing a few tutorials, I settled upon Google Calendar and Schedule Once. I've been using both ever since. Don't overthink this step in the process, but do take some time to conduct your own research and make a choice that feels right.

Once you choose a calendar and scheduling system, it becomes quite integrated in your life and will be a hassle to unwind, so take the time to make the best decision you can with the information you have, commit, and move on to the next step in your common path to uncommon success.

2. With what frequency will you deliver your content?

Now that I had my calendar and scheduler locked in, it was time to decide the frequency with which I was going to deliver my content. I had decided *Entrepreneurs on Fire* would be published seven days a week, but that still left a lot of decisions to be made.

- **Show Notes.** Was I going to create a show notes page for every episode or do one weekly roundup of all seven shows?
- **Email.** I was planning on building an email list and had to decide the frequency of the broadcasts I would send.
- **Social Media.** What social media platforms would I use to promote the show and how often would I publish on my chosen platforms?

I decided to keep it simple and add more complexity in the future as my team grew and systems were dialed in.

- **Show Notes.** Since *Entrepreneurs on Fire* was the focus of my business, I decided that a show notes page would be created and published with every episode. This would give my listeners a place to go for recaps, links, and more information. It would also give me the chance to increase the visits to my website so I could grow my email list and the overall value I was providing my listeners.
- **Email.** I decided on two emails per week, one focusing on the episodes I had created and another just focused on a topic I thought would be relevant to my audience.

- **Social Media.** I decided to start with one daily tweet promoting that day's episode, plus two Facebook posts per week with teasers of the shows.

Now that I knew the frequency of my content, it was time to take the next step in the creation of my content production plan.

3. Which days will your content be delivered?

This part of my content production plan was straightforward. *Entrepreneurs on Fire* would be seven days a week, so there was no room for overthinking which days of the week I would release each episode. The only consideration I had was at what time of day I would release each episode.

I knew most of my listener base would be in the United States of America. I also knew my avatar would be listening while on his commute to work.

I went to Google and searched *earliest time New Yorkers begin their morning commute.* After reading a few articles, I found that 5:00 a.m. was the consensus and decided to back it up one hour and release my episodes at 4:00 a.m.

In my mind, my avatar would wake up in the morning and while he was brewing his morning cup of coffee he would load up the most recent *Entrepreneurs on Fire* episode before giving his wife and kids a sad kiss goodbye, jumping in the car, and heading out to a twenty-fivish-minute commute to his place of work.

Not to get too deep in the weeds, but I also had to make sure the episode wasn't released too early; otherwise it would show up as yesterday's episode for West Coasters. For example, if I published the episodes at 2:30 a.m. Eastern, it would be 11:30 p.m. Pacific. Be careful not to overthink things like this, but at the same time doing the little things right can add up big over time.

I knew my avatar was looking for a fresh episode delivered to him every day and I wanted him to see that fresh episode, time stamped with today's date, delivered to him every day.

I synced the publishing of the show notes with the release of the podcast episodes, so the only remaining decisions to make were which days I would publish my email newsletter and social media.

For my email newsletter, I would be sending out two per week and had to decide on the when and the what. After some consideration, I decided on a Monday newsletter sharing the upcoming episodes for the week, as well as some key takeaways and lessons learned from the prior week's shows. This would get my audience excited about the episodes that were ahead, as well provide usefulness in the form of value bombs that had been dropped the week prior.

For the second newsletter, I decided on a Friday email to recap the week's shows, tease the weekend episodes, and share one massive *a-ha* moment I had personally experienced over the past five days. This would give my audience a chance to reflect on the content over the previous five days, make a note to listen to any they missed that sounded appealing, get excited for the weekend shows—and of course get value from the incredible knowledge shared by my guests.

Now that my email newsletter had a structure in place, it was time to firm up my plan for social media. I had already committed to a tweet a day, but when would I send that tweet? I used a tool that showed when my followers were most active on the platform and chose a time in that range. My tweets were simply a quick teaser of that day's episode with a link to the show notes.

For my twice-per-week Facebook posts, I decided on Wednesday and Sunday. Wednesday was nicely tucked in between my Monday and Friday newsletter, and Sunday was a day I found my followers spent a significant amount of time on Facebook by using a similar tool I had used for my Twitter audience. As for the specific content, I decided to keep things simple and highlight one episode with my top takeaways, and a link to that show.

Suddenly, my content production plan was taking shape. My overwhelm evaporated. I could look at my calendar and see when I was going to create, what I was going to create, and when I was going to publish. With a plan in place, all I had to do was execute and my content production plan would become a value-delivering machine.

It was time for the next step in the process.

One side note I want to make about my social media plan. I launched Entrepreneurs on Fire *in 2012, so I am sharing what made sense in the social media space then. I would encourage you to use the plan I created as a guide and to choose the social media platforms that make the most sense for your avatar at the time you are creating your content production plan.*

4. What is the average length of content you will create?

Now it was time to decide the length of the content I would create. This is where the work you put in during chapter 3 really begins to pay off. When you know exactly what your avatar needs, these types of questions become fill-in-the-blanks. At every fork in the road, remember to ask yourself what your avatar would want. Allow your avatar to be your guide along the common path to uncommon success.

My avatar (Jimmy) has a twenty-five-minute commute to work every morning and a thirty-five-minute commute home in the evening (he gets stuck in a little rush-hour traffic). Therefore, I decided every *Entrepreneurs on Fire* would be between twenty and thirty minutes. My goal was to allow Jimmy to start and finish an episode on a single commute in the morning, and catch up on any missed episodes (or relisten to his favorites) on his evening commute home.

My twenty- to thirty-minute episode length was a guide, as I was not going to cut off Tony Robbins when he decided to give me fifty-three minutes of his time for a show (true story). However, I wanted my listeners to have certain expectations when they pressed *play* on an *Entrepreneurs on Fire* episode: high audio quality, high energy, high value, and most shows in the twenty- to thirty-minute range.

I wanted to bring the same congruency to the other content I was creating. Remember, you're not implementing a rigid set of principles you'll never deviate from, but instead a set of guidelines that will help you maintain focus and consistency in your message and content creation.

For my show notes, I decided upon a system where I would have the top section be the three biggest value bombs dropped during the show, followed by the links that were mentioned throughout the interview. The final section would be my biggest takeaway. This system allowed me to create quality show notes in a reasonable amount of time while ensuring that my listeners knew they could expect value when they visited our website.

For email, I kept things simple. My one requirement was a maximum of five hundred words per email. I knew Jimmy had limited free time and that it was important to deliver a value-packed email in a clear and concise manner.

Besides the word limit, I left a lot of room for artistic creativity within my newsletters and over the years have tried a lot of different experiments, some of which worked great and others of which flopped miserably. As with everything, I've kept the great and dropped the flops.

For social media, I took a similar approach as I did with email. I implemented a hundred-word limit per social media post and left a lot of room for experiments and such.

As with everything along the common path to uncommon success, I always followed the process below:

Create → Publish → Request feedback → Analyze the feedback → Implement adjustments → Repeat.

5. How much time will it take you to create each piece of content?

For most of my childhood, I was a basketball player. By the third grade, I was getting good. When I entered junior high, I became the starting point guard. My sophomore year of high school, I was announced as the starting point guard for varsity. I steadily improved over the next two years, and by the time my senior season rolled around, I was poised to become All-State.

Sadly, it was never meant to be. During a summer basketball camp, I developed patella tendinitis in both knees. It never healed and forced me to miss the fall soccer season. I tested out my knees in the first few basketball practices, but it was obvious they were not healed, and with tears in my eyes I told my coach I was out. It was an incredibly difficult decision, but at the same time a small relief as I knew how painful it would have been had I continued.

Being a three-sport athlete, this would be the first time I wouldn't be spending all my free time at practices and games. With all this free time, I began to get quite bored. School finished up at 2:00 p.m. What was I supposed to do for the next eight hours while all my friends were off playing games?

That's when I received a letter from the father of our school's star swimmer. He gave his condolences for my lost senior basketball season and then reminded me that I had grown up on a lake, swimming all summer long. Also, I had swum competitively at a very young age, prior to basketball taking over my winter schedule. My father had been a collegiate swimmer at Georgetown, so swimming competitively was "in my genes."

I talked it over with my Dad and decided this was a great way to stay in shape, stay out of trouble, and potentially have a little success in the high school swimming scene.

For lack of a better word, I started off the swim season like a fish out of water. I refused to wear Speedos (basketball players only rock the baggiest of baggy shorts), I had no idea how to do a flip turn, and I was terrible off the starting blocks. On top of all that, the only stroke I was competent at was freestyle, the most competitive stroke in swimming. Despite it all, I knew I had to give it a go.

Our first swim meet was not a disaster, but close to it. I swam the 50-yard free, which is like the 100-meter sprint in track. It's an all-out sprint of two pool laps. I stepped onto the blocks as the only competitor not wearing a Speedo. My bright yellow swim trunks must have looked obnoxious. When the starter pistol cracked, I was last off the blocks.

I probably made up a little time in the first lap, but lost it all when I was the only one not to execute a flip turn. I grabbed the wall with both my hands, lost all my momentum, took a deep breath, and pushed off for the final twenty-five yards. After about twenty yards, I was out of gas, and couldn't believe I hadn't finished yet.

I literally stopped, started treading water, looked around, and saw that everyone else had in fact finished. Some were already out of the pool toweling off. I somehow splashed my way the final five yards, touched the wall, and completed my first high school swim race.

What happened next changed everything for me. I looked up at the scoreboard and saw my time. It was bad: 33:04.

But something inside me clicked. I had done so many things wrong, but now I had a barometer to measure my progress. A fire was lit, and for the rest of the swim season, it never went out.

Every day at practice, I committed to working on one weak area of my swim game until it became a strength.

Flip turns were my first focus. Thirty minutes before practice and thirty minutes after, I worked on nothing else. As days turned into weeks, I slowly but surely improved my flip turn. Then one day it just clicked. I knew exactly the moment to go into my flip, how hard to kick off the wall, and how long to stay underwater to maximize speed.

Having conquered the flip, I moved onto my next weakness, the starting block. I practiced my foot placement, I learned to anticipate the starting gun, I perfected how I entered the water and how long I stayed under before surfacing to begin my freestyle strokes.

Then I moved onto improving the length of my stroke, then the method of my kicks, and then how to most effectively breathe while maintaining a streamlined posture.

As the swim meets came and went, I was fired up to see my times go lower and lower. Each improvement shaved seconds off my times. Soon, I wasn't finishing last.

Then it happened. I finished third in a race, which netted my team some points that helped propel us to victory.

I knew the time had come. It was time to shed my baggy swim trunks and become a real competitive simmer. Those swim trunks had given me the courage to take the first step, but now they were figuratively (and literally!) weighing me down and holding me back. The drag on baggy swim trunks is obnoxious.

We were about to compete against the top swimming school in the state, one that my high school had never beaten before. They had a strong team and a very fast swimmer for the 50-yard freestyle. I kept the towel around my waist till the last second, but when the announcer said the words "swimmers, take your mark," I shed the towel and stepped up to the racing blocks.

I felt like everyone must be staring at me, but of course it was all a figment of my imagination. I was simply one of eight swimmers, all of whom were wearing Speedos.

The pistol cracked and everything fell into place. The perfect start. The perfect strokes, strong kicks, and streamlined breathing.

I could see out of the corner of my eye I was keeping pace with their top swimmer! It was all going to come down to the flip turn.

Three, two, one, *flip*!

Boom! Nailed it.

Now it was a sprint to the end. When my hand hit the wall, I knew I had just set a personal best, but was it enough?

I looked up at the scoreboard and saw a magical number next to my name: 1. I had done it!

I had swum a personal best, I had beaten their top swimmer, and I had scored the most points possible for my team.

My final time was quite fitting: 23:04.

In all those months of work, I had shaved exactly ten seconds off my first race. I felt incredibly proud.

I went on to finish first in our state finals in the 50-yard freestyle and took third place in the 100. That experience showed me the power of focus. I knew there were six areas where my swimming needed vast improvement. If I had tried to tackle them all at once, I would have been overwhelmed, frustrated, and I would have failed.

By tackling one struggle at a time, everything felt doable. I could see and feel my progress each week. Over the course of the season, I vastly improved in each of those six areas, one step at a time.

I'm sharing this story with you because this is a period in my life I refer to often when I feel overwhelmed in my business. When I feel like there is simply too much to do and too little time to do it, I remind myself that the common path to uncommon success is a journey. It's a journey that requires patience, persistence, and focus. My days of competitive swimming are long gone, but the lessons I learned from my senior season will stay with me a lifetime.

It's time to explain the title of this section: *How much time will each piece of content take you to create?*

At first, it will take you a long time. It will take a lot of brainpower, energy, and bandwidth. It is always this way when you start something new.

But each time you create a new piece of content, you'll get better, you'll become more efficient, you'll create systems and processes. Just like how I focused on one deficient part of my swim skills one at a time, you'll focus on one part of your deficient content creation system. Don't get discouraged and overwhelmed when round one takes a long time.

It won't take as long in round two. By round twenty, you'll have a chuckle remembering how you used to do it.

A common struggle podcasters have is when they edit their show for the first time. *John, I finished my first interview and it went great! But then I spent three hours editing the twenty-minute interview. There's no way I can spend that much time on every interview going forward.*

My response is always the same. *Of course it took you three hours. It's your first time editing a podcast episode and everything is new and confusing. It took me three hours to edit my first interview and I was terrified as I knew there was no way I could keep up that pace for a daily show. But my tenth time editing took ninety minutes. My fiftieth time took thirty. Now, over 2,500 episodes in, each interview takes me three to five minutes to edit, and I do a better job than I did the first time. How? I got a little bit better each time. I improved one aspect of my system or process. You will too. Have faith, stay consistent, and focus on getting one small step better every time. You got this!*

To wrap this up, it will take you a long time to create your first piece of content, so plan accordingly. But feel confident that every time you create, you'll improve a part of the process. You'll get faster, better, and more efficient. The common path to uncommon success is about doing the little things right over a long period of time.

Let's go!

6. How far in advance will you create the content that is going to be published?

Those who are *not* on the common path to uncommon success constantly find themselves in a "create on demand" cycle. They are always rushing to meet their goals before they miss a deadline.

The result for the person consuming the content? The content feels hurried. It feels watered down. It feels like there is something missing.

The life of the creator of the content? The creator is constantly stressed, anxious, and feeling like their back is against the wall.

That is not our path. Those on the common path to uncommon success have a much different experience. We take comfort in knowing our plan is in place. We take pride that everything is working in harmony.

The result for the person consuming the content? The content feels well structured. It feels whole. It delivers on the promise of massive value.

The life of the creator of the content? The creator feels accomplished. They feel empowered. They feel in control and ahead of the game.

When I committed to the audacious goal of publishing a podcast every single day, I had to deliver on that commitment. I knew there would be a lot of hurdles. First was finding enough qualified entrepreneurs to interview. Second was getting their contact information.

Then, I would have to convince them to dedicate thirty minutes of their day chatting with a person they had never met before on a podcast they had never heard of before.

When I finally got a yes, I'd still need 364 more yeses for the year.

I knew if *Entrepreneurs on Fire* was going to work, I needed to get forty-five days ahead and stay there. That meant my goal was to always have forty-five episodes "in the can." That way, if I had a wave of cancellations, the power went out on interview day, or any other natural or unnatural disaster cropped up, I would have a buffer in place to see me through.

I spent the three months before I launched getting these forty-five episodes done and dusted. Once I launched, I followed a schedule that always kept me at least thirty to forty-five days ahead of the game.

2017 tested that buffer . . .

As the category 5 hurricane Maria barreled toward my home island of Puerto Rico, I knew it was time to depart. Luckily, my buffer was in place and *Entrepreneurs on Fire* never missed a day.

I'll never forget recording *EOF* episodes with a handheld mic by a pool at our Airbnb in Tampa. I had to battle mosquitoes and crappy Wi-Fi, but I completed the interviews because, as they say, the show must go on!

When you are coming up with your ideal, don't let the number forty-five intimidate you. That is for a daily podcast. I recommend having forty-five days of content as a buffer, so if you're creating a weekly video, that's just creating a six-video buffer. A little less intimidating, am I right?

Before I close this section, I want to share a common question I receive on this topic: "John, how did you find all those guests before *Entrepreneurs on Fire* was a hit?"

My strategy is specific to finding guests for your podcast, but the concept can be applied across most platforms. First, I asked myself the following question: "Where are successful and inspiring entrepreneurs being featured?" I started a list, and at the top were two very promising opportunities, business magazines and business conferences.

The first one was easy. I simply subscribed to the digital version of some of the top business magazines and went through their archives, making note of all the entrepreneurs they featured.

Then the real work began.

To be featured in a top-flight business magazine, you were doing a lot of things right. This type of exposure meant a lot of people were competing for your attention. I did my research on which social media platforms they were most active on, followed them, and began to engage with their content daily.

One thing I found out quickly was that people pay attention. Just because they have a lot of followers doesn't mean they ignore their comments and messages. They notice, and once you become a committed and active follower, you are significantly increasing your chances of a *yes* when you make your ask because you've been a person of value in their world and that matters.

Now that I've achieved a certain level of success, I can speak from firsthand experience. Most of the messages I receive begin with a version of *"Hi John, I'm sure you get thousands of these messages and have a whole team answering these but . . ."* The reality is, because everyone thinks I receive tons of messages daily, few send them, and as a result, I can respond to every message I receive personally.

Back when I was sending messages to dream guests for *Entrepreneurs on Fire*, I experienced this firsthand when I emailed Seth Godin. Within the hour he responded with, "How does 1:00 p.m. Eastern tomorrow work for you?"

My jaw dropped to the floor and I don't think I've ever canceled a dentist appointment so fast.

I hope you take this advice and engage with those you want to connect with. I'm not saying you will bat 1.000, but it will be worth your time and effort.

The next strategy I used was pure gold and proved that a daily podcast was possible.

I googled *best entrepreneur conferences this year*. Searching through the results, I compiled a list of over fifty conferences. My next step was *not* to buy the event ticket, a plane ticket, and book a hotel room. Not even close. Instead, I simply visited the event's website, clicked on the tab labeled *speakers*, and presto, a list of the speakers appeared, along with their bio, speaking topic, and personal website.

My next step was to create a list of my dream speakers using this information and start contacting them one by one. Once I found a person who I thought would be a great guest, I clicked the link to their website, clicked on their contact form, and composed the following message:

Hello XXX,

My name is John Lee Dumas and I host a business podcast called *Entrepreneurs on Fire.* I interview the world's most successful and inspiring entrepreneurs seven days a week.

I believe you would be the perfect fit for my show, and I would be honored if you would join me for a thirty-minute, audio-only, online interview from the comfort of your own home (no need to comb your hair or even wear pants!).

I saw you are presenting on XXX topic at the XXX conference, and I think that topic would be a perfect fit for my audience, Fire Nation.

If you are interested, please click the link below and choose a time that works for you.

If none of those times work, please reply with a couple days and times that do work and I will be sure to accommodate your schedule.

Thank you for taking the time to read this, and prepare to ignite!

—John Lee Dumas

Even before my podcast launched, I had a 60 percent response rate and a 40 percent success rate. That meant four out of every ten messages I sent resulted in the booking of a perfect guest for my show!

The key to this success was that I made it easy for them to say *yes.* Let me repeat that. The key to this success was that I made it easy for them to say *yes*. My request was for them to talk about a topic they were an expert on from the comfort of their own home.

Always remember, fortune favors the bold. Put in the work, make the ask, and you'll be surprised at the level of your success!

7. What days will you set aside each week for content creation?

When I hired my mentor and joined a mastermind, I set myself up for success. My mentor was where I wanted to be and could guide me through the pitfalls and ensure I focused on what mattered. My mastermind consisted of ten other podcasters at various stages in their podcasting journey, including the podcast answer man himself (Cliff Ravenscraft) leading the way.

However, there was one consistent piece of advice I received from everyone.

Don't attempt a daily podcast. You will fail. You'll run out of guests. You'll run out of time. You'll run out of gas. Your listeners will fall behind, get frustrated, and unsubscribe. There are reasons why a daily podcast interviewing successful entrepreneurs does not exist—it would never work!

This advice did not faze me. In fact, it *fired* me up. If some of the most successful podcasters in the world were telling me it couldn't be done and I could find a way to do it, *wow*, what an opportunity!

I've always loved the quote *the higher the obstacle, the lower the competition*. I knew if I could find a way to create a daily podcast interviewing the world's most successful entrepreneurs, I would own that space. I knew if I went the extra mile, there would be no competition.

> There are no traffic jams on the extra mile.
> —ZIG ZIGLAR

I knew *Entrepreneurs on Fire* wasn't for everyone, but I knew there were people who desperately wanted to wake up every morning with an interview from an inspiring entrepreneur. I knew if I could figure out how to produce a daily show, I would be the only option and over time I would create a show worthy of my listeners' ears.

So, I sat down to figure it out. Why was everyone so adamant that a daily podcast would never work? That's when it hit me. They were picturing me getting up every morning, scheduling an interview, hosting that interview, editing that interview, writing the show notes page, publishing that interview, and then creating the social media to go with it.

That schedule meant I would be spending my entire day publishing and marketing one episode. What if one thing went wrong? What if I got sick? What if my guest got sick? What if the power went out? What if? What it? What if?

Thinking about it that way, it was terrifying and I could see why I the top podcasters in the industry were giving me that advice. If a daily show was going to happen, I'd have to figure out a better way.

That's when it hit me, again. What if, instead of doing one episode every single day, I did eight interviews one day a week?

I would schedule each interview for one hour, plenty of buffer for my twenty- to thirty-minute episodes. Then, in eight hours, I would have eight episodes done and dusted. Enough for a full week, plus one for good measure.

When I brought this idea up to my mastermind, they thought I was crazy. Eight interviews in one day? You'll be exhausted! I did not disagree; it was a lot of work. But I recalled the sixteen-hour days I put in while on my tour of duty in Iraq. I thought of the heat, the dust, the danger.

Was sitting in my air-conditioned home office for eight hours once a week chatting with inspiring entrepreneurs really that crazy? The obvious answer was *no*. What if I looked at each interview day as my "Super Bowl"?

Yes, the day would be long and demanding. But the sun would set at the end of the day and I'd have eight interviews recorded, and it would feel great. I bought into this Super Bowl approach hook, line, and sinker.

With this new perspective and commitment, my next step was to choose the day I would host these interviews. After giving it some thought, I settled upon Tuesday. I would use Monday to get things in order and fully prepped. Tuesday would be my Super Bowl, and the remainder of the week was rest, recoup, and focus on all the other parts of my business that needed attending.

For over 2,500 episodes, this style of batching has treated me well. I implemented this form of batching in every part of my business. Tuesdays were interview days. Wednesdays were for editing, show notes creation, and scheduling the episodes. Thursdays were reserved for miscellaneous tasks that were on my to-do list. Fridays were dedicated to creating the following week's social media and email broadcasts. Weekends were for relaxing, recharging, and knocking out a few tasks if the opportunity arose. Mondays were focused on setting the tone for the week and ensuring I was totally prepared for what was to come.

I came to refer to this as "batching like a baller," and I loved it. Over the years, as we've added team members and refined systems and processes, my weekly schedule has evolved, but the one thing I have never changed is the batching of our content on specific days.

It allows me to do what others in the podcasting space thought impossible: deliver a daily podcast two thousand days in a row, generate over eighty-five million downloads, and create a life of financial freedom and fulfillment.

8. Who is holding you accountable to your content creation plan?

The mastermind I joined at the beginning of my entrepreneurial journey proved to be a great decision. When I shared my vision of a daily podcast, every single member of the mastermind tried to talk me out of it. However, once they saw I was determined to commit to my vision, they became incredibly supportive. And, if I'm being honest, their initial doubt was fuel for my fire.

Every week, our mastermind would meet, share our wins from the previous seven days, ask for guidance and support on our current struggles, and set a goal for the following week. Each week, I set audacious goals.

All the magic happens outside of your comfort zone.
–ANONYMOUS

All my goals were outside of my comfort zone. I respected everyone in my mastermind. We were all chasing our dreams, putting ourselves out there, and working our booties off. Something special happens when a group like that comes together. You don't want to let each other down. You reach farther than you thought possible and fly higher than you previously dreamed.

I remember multiple times when our mastermind was meeting the following day and I had yet to complete the goal I had set the week prior. If it had just been me, I would have pushed back the deadline. But it wasn't just me. There were nine other people who had set goals the week prior, worked hard all week to accomplish them, and were counting on me to do the same.

I pictured sharing my reason for not accomplishing the goal in the mastermind. I wouldn't get any sympathy. I wouldn't receive under-standing head nods. None of that. I'd get probing questions as to why I failed in accomplishing the one goal I had set for the week.

Knowing what awaited me, I would suck it up, buckle down, and accomplish my goal! Over the entire year, I never missed a self-imposed deadline for my content creation plan. I created a plan of action, shared that plan with my mastermind, and saw progress week over week.

It's amazing what you can accomplish when you have a group of people holding you accountable every week. You need that. Why? It's easy to lose your momentum. It's easy to lose your way. It's easy to sub-mit to overwhelm. It's easy to fade away into the entrepreneurial abyss.

Your mastermind is your lifeline. They can be your rock: the place you go to complain, to share your fears, to unload your worries. The place you go to ask questions, to ask for guidance, to request feedback.

They are experiencing the same emotions and have the same questions. Just as you need them, they need you. The warmth and joy you'll feel while helping others as they struggle will add to your fuel. You are all in this together.

Those on the common path to uncommon success have accountability partners to ensure you are sticking to your content creation plan. Chapter 6 was focused on this aspect of your journey, so please refer to that as your guide to create or join your perfect mastermind.

You got this!

9. **What day of the month will you set aside to evaluate your content production plan to adjust as needed?**

As I shared earlier, our AARs (After-Action Reviews) were one of the most valuable things we did in the Army. We were the best military force in the world and made a myriad of mistakes. These AARs allowed us to reflect on our mistakes, adjust our actions, and improve our processes so we would become better and more effective going forward.

As entrepreneurs, we need to do the same at least once a month. Personally, I choose the last Friday of every month. I block off four hours on my calendar for these After-Action Reviews, ensuring it will always happen. For the entire month leading up to this final Friday, whenever I finish a project or think I have something worthy to add, I open the AAR calendar invite and add it to a list of items that will be a part of that month's review. When the time comes, I open my calendar invite and work through each item one by one.

Over the years, I've developed the below set of questions to assist my AARs:

1. What was the goal of this project?
2. Did I accomplish the goal?

3. What went well?
4. What went poorly?
5. What did I learn from this project?
6. Does this project align with the core values of my business?
7. Will I do something like this again?
8. What would I do differently next time?
9. What systems and processes can I put in place to improve execution?
10. Is this a project I need to dedicate my personal time to or can I delegate this to someone on my team or an independent contractor?
11. What specific value did this add to my business?
12. Who else is doing projects like these that I can study and learn from?

Below is a real-world example of how I conducted a successful AAR.

1. **What was the goal of this project?** To host my first webinar promoting my brand-new podcasting course, Podcasters' Paradise.
2. **Did I accomplish the goal?** Yes, I ran the webinar successfully. Over 150 people participated in the training and fourteen people purchased Podcasters' Paradise.
3. **What went well?** The delivery of my keynote presentation went very well. I provided a lot of value and felt it was a smooth delivery.
4. **What went poorly?** My interaction with the attendees in the live chat. There were a lot of great conversations and questions happening but I was too nervous and focused on the presentation and ignored the comments. This is a missed opportunity, as engaging the attendees is a great way to build rapport and remove barriers to purchase.
5. **What did I learn from this project?** I learned that webinars are going to be a great way to provide massive value about

podcasting, as well as an amazing opportunity to present
the opportunity for people to join Podcasters' Paradise.

6. **Does this project align with the core values of my business?**
Absolutely. Providing free, valuable, and consistent content
is what we do at *Entrepreneurs on Fire*.

7. **Will I do something like this again?** If people keep showing
up, I will host this training at least twice a month.

8. **What would I do differently next time?** I would have Kate
(more about her soon) moderate the chat and send me
the important and relevant questions people have so I'm
able to reply to each one.

9. **What systems and processes can I put in place to improve
execution?** I'm going to improve our email sequence so
attendees have all the information they need prior to the
webinar. There were a lot of questions that could have
been answered prior to the webinar, allowing the attendees
to focus on the content.

10. **Is this a project I need to be lead on or can I delegate this
to someone on my team or an independent contractor?** I
need to be the lead on this project. It is important for me
to be the one delivering the training, improving my
presentation skills, answering the questions, and
engaging with the attendees. I will bring my team in to
handle other parts of the process, but I will remain the
lead on this.

11. **What specific value did this add to my business?** This
webinar adds another opportunity to deliver the free value
to my audience, increasing their trust of our business. It
also positions me as an industry expert in the podcasting
space while adding great exposure to our premium
podcasting community, Podcasters' Paradise.

12. **Who else is doing projects like these I can study and learn
from?** Lewis Howes and Russell Brunson are masters at
webinars. I will register for their trainings and study the

entire process to see what improvements I can add to our current setup.

The above was just one of the multiple AARs I did on this specific Friday.

As you can imagine, doing AARs allows you to understand what is working in your business, how to improve upon it, and if it makes sense, how to double down. It was through these AARs that I realized just how true the 80/20 rule is: 80 percent of your revenue and impact will come from 20 percent of your activities. Doing monthly AARs will help you identify and improve the 20 percent, turning your business into a lean, mean, revenue-generating machine!

An Entrepreneur on Fire's Path to Uncommon Success

KATE ERICKSON ON CREATING A CONTENT PRODUCTION PLAN

If you're too busy to build good systems, then you'll always be too busy. —BRIAN LOGUE

KATE FOUND HER dream job. After years of slugging it out in the HR department of a bank, Kate finally had a job she loved. She was an account executive at a boutique advertising and marketing agency.

Kate had seen *Mad Men* (twice) and knew she was in for a high-octane, challenging, and fulfilling adventure. For a while, it was everything she hoped it would be. Until it wasn't.

Kate was handed the company's largest client, and knowing the importance of the relationship, she tried to do everything she could to keep the client happy. But it wasn't easy, and eventually her patience and love for her work started to fade.

When her boyfriend, John (*me!*), asked her to join his fledgling podcast company, she initially declined. She was learning so much at the agency and really wanted to prove that she could handle the long hours and unrealistic deadlines being thrown at her. But when I asked again three months later, in 2013, she realized the agency life she was trying to create through her rose-colored glasses had to be put to rest. This was an opportunity she couldn't pass up twice.

I knew Kate had a talent for details and organization, so I put her in charge of creating the systems and processes that would be the engine of *Entrepreneurs on Fire*. Kate sat down and created the first version of the content production plan. One year later, *Entrepreneurs on Fire* was a multimillion-dollar-a-year business. Kate's next adventure had officially begun.

Fast-forward to 2014. Kate had been working on *Entrepreneurs on Fire*'s content production plan for over a year and it was time to put it to the test. For the first time since launch day back in 2012, we were going to take a vacation. The vacation would consist of multiple European stops over the course of two weeks. Our goal? Completely unplug from the business, trusting our team to handle everything.

Kate created a special Gmail account that was only to be used by our team in case of emergency. With some anxiety and trepidation, we boarded the plane and said goodbye to the day-to-day operations of *Entrepreneurs on Fire*.

Fast-forward two weeks and the trip was an absolute success. The emergency Gmail account remained undisturbed and the business was still thriving. Kate realized she had an opportunity to integrate our "vacation content production plan" into our daily operations.

Each subsequent year, we extended our vacations by fifteen days. In 2015, we took a thirty-day vacation. In 2016, we bumped it up to forty-five, enjoyed sixty days in 2017, and a full seventy-five days in 2018. We really tested the limits in 2019 when we took a ninety-day vacation that circled the globe, leaving from Puerto Rico, hitting Colorado, Fiji, Eastern Europe, and Western Europe before finally returning home to Puerto Rico.

All the while, our business continued to generate six figures of net profit every month, all because our systems, processes, and content production plan were flawless. Here are Kate's seven keys to creating a successful content production plan:

1. **Know your topic.** What specifically are you going to focus on/create content around? This should be based on your passions/expertise (Zone of Fire) and what you've confirmed your avatar wants/needs.

2. **Set a goal.** Every piece of content should have a goal and CTA that tells your audience what step to take next. Whether it's a blog post, podcast episode, social media post, video . . . make it easy for your audience to take the next step with you.

3. **Choose a medium.** Ideally, you're focusing on *one* medium at a time. Once you've created a full content plan for that medium, you can look to expand. For example, if you're interested in starting a blog and a podcast, choose one to launch first, get your content plan in place, and then add the other once things are running smoothly. A good way to determine which medium is best for you is to first ask, "Where is my avatar hanging out? What would they want to consume?" And a great way to test out different media is through repurposing. Once you've landed on *one* medium, make sure you're leveraging that content across several platforms. Identify potential focus areas based on how much a medium moves the needle.

4. **Establish frequency and length.** Consistency is key, so early on you should be establishing a frequency: How often will you publish? Be honest with yourself about what you have time to commit to, and be sure to consider what your avatar would want. Daily might feel overwhelming to them. A blog post that takes twenty minutes to read might be too much. Be sure to consider this when establishing your frequency and length.

5. **Create a format.** Whether it's a template, outline, or checklist, put one in place early. For example, every time I create a podcast episode, I have a bank of content ideas I go to. This ensures that I never sit down to create and spin my wheels trying to decide what I should talk about. Then, I have the same intro, the same music, and the same "hello" every time. Next, I introduce the topic we'll discuss, walk through a set of steps related to that topic, and then recap. My outro is the same every time, followed by my call to action. Having a template, outline, or checklist in place you can pull up every time you go to create content makes it super easy to dive right into creating. And this goes for any medium: blogs, podcasts, videos, social media posts—the possibilities for creating a format you can follow every time are endless!

6. **Get feedback.** Once you've started publishing content, be sure to ask your audience for feedback! This is a critical step in figuring out what's working, what could be improved, and what you might want to test. Asking for feedback can come in many forms—it might even be your CTA for certain pieces of content. Something as simple as "I'd love to hear your #1 takeaway from today's episode! Shoot me an email and let me know!" Or you might ask for feedback via social media in response to comments or messages your audience is sending you. Another great option: request feedback in response to emails or other types of outreach you receive from listeners.

7. **Put your plan in place.** Schedule it! Now that you have a solid foundation, it's time to put it all together into a scheduled plan. Sit down and map out what it will take for you to put a plan in place that always keeps you one month ahead of schedule. So, if you're producing a weekly podcast, your overall plan might look something like this:

- Monday, 9:00 a.m. to 11:00 a.m.: Prepare content for four episodes.
- Tuesday, 9:00 a.m. to 11:00 a.m.: Record four episodes.
- Wednesday, 9:00 a.m. to 11:00 a.m.: Edit and upload four episodes and schedule out social media.

If you were to stick to this plan, you would always be one month ahead on your content with just six hours, spread across three days, *one* time per month! Your plan will look different based on your schedule, but if you stick to it on a consistent basis, you'll never have to worry about falling behind on your content creation again. And that means more time to work on growing and scaling your business! In Kate's own words: "Our content production plan has ensured that *EOFire's* audience has consistently grown over the years with very little paid advertising, which has allowed us to increase the level of freedom and fulfillment we have in our life and business."

Thank you, Kate Erickson.

You can learn more about Kate at EOFire.com/about.

Check out your free companion course for added support along *The Common Path to Uncommon Success*: EOFire.com/success-course.

CHAPTER 8

Create Content

Content isn't king, it's the kingdom.
—LEE ODDEN

Your content production plan is in place. Now it's time to do the work. Sadly, "doing the work" is the hardest part, which is why most entrepreneurs never celebrate their one-year anniversary.

It's exciting to have an idea. It's fun to share your idea with others. It's wonderful to envision your idea changing the world and creating a life of financial freedom and fulfillment for you and your loved ones.

It's another thing entirely to sit down, day after day, week after week, month after month . . . and do the work. The trifecta for the common path to uncommon success is producing free, valuable, and consistent content. What's the hardest part of the trifecta? Being *consistent*.

Most people can sit down one time and create a very valuable piece of content. Most people can do it twice. Heck, I've seen thousands of people do it for a month straight.

But what separates the entrepreneurs who fade into obscurity and those who find uncommon success? *Consistency*. Not for a week. Not for a month. But for years.

It's hard to remain consistent for that length of time, and it's easy to stop. If your *why* is not strong enough, you'll stop too. Everyone has a different why and it's critical to identify yours early and often.

A question I asked every guest for the first two thousand episodes was, "Share with us your *a-ha* moment, the moment you had an idea that really took off and led to the success you are now experiencing today." It didn't click with me at first, but after the fortieth or so time of my guest mentioning a specific event in their life that coincided with their *a-ha* moment, my own light bulb went off.

Can you guess what that life event was? They had a baby.

At first it seemed so counterintuitive. Wouldn't a baby throw your life into chaos? Wouldn't you have less time, not more? Wouldn't you have every excuse in the world *not* to do the work?

I knew I had to dig deeper.

What I found was, *yes*, a baby could throw your life into chaos, take up an incredible amount of time, and give you every excuse in the world to abandon your work. But the one thing a baby will give you is your *why*.

It's important to remember that, at our core, we are all human beings. It is natural to have doubt, fear, stress, and anxiety when we try something new, especially when that something new might not work.

That doubt, fear, stress, and anxiety has kept us alive for tens of thousands of years. It's why our ancestors didn't go for an aimless jungle stroll at night and get devoured by a saber-toothed tiger but instead stayed huddled in caves with fire and companionship. They stayed alive, they reproduced, they passed along their doubt, fear, stress, and anxiety, and now you are reading these words today.

What's my point? My point is, it is normal to experience these emotions, and when your why is not strong enough, you'll find excuses to avoid doing the things that trigger these feelings.

As honest as your intentions are to do the work, thousands of years of doubt, fear, stress, and anxiety will try to hold you back. Those emotions want to protect you from becoming vulnerable by trying something new and scary. They want you to stay the course of what is safe and secure.

Creating a life of financial freedom and fulfillment requires you to get out of your comfort zone. It requires you to embrace the emotions of doubt, fear, stress, and anxiety and rise above them. It's the only way you'll be able to push through the fear and create the content you need to achieve uncommon success and impact people around the world.

Back to the baby effect. It's scary to sit down, face your fears, and do the work. What's scarier? Not providing for your newborn.

Those emails you haven't been sending? Sent. Those podcasts and videos you haven't recorded because "you don't like the sound of your voice"? Done and done. The outline for your first online course you can't seem to get started? Finished in an hour.

How is all this possible? For so many reasons, but mostly for the following. It is now scarier *not* to do what it takes to find uncommon success. It is scarier *not* to provide a solid financial foundation for your newborn than it is making cold calls to prospective clients.

Before, you didn't have your why so you defaulted to the easier option, not doing the work. Now you default to your *only* option, doing the work.

And the fact that you have less time now? That's a good thing. It's called Parkinson's law. *Tasks will expand to the time allotted.* When you had all day to do one thing, you procrastinated all day, because you had all day. When you have one hour to do *all* the things, you sit down, your brain drops into *focus* mode, and you do the work. All the work.

So why did so many of my guests' *a-ha* moment coincide with the birth of their child? Before that life-changing event, they were lacking their why and simply not doing the work. They were floating along humming the words "someday this will all come together." The birth of their child took someday and made it *today*. All the excuses went out the window. The doubt, fear, stress, and anxiety of doing the work was now focused on their baby, and doing the work became a priority.

Now I'm not saying go and have a baby, but what I am saying is that you need to find your why. You need to find a reason to do the work that is bigger than just doing the work, and when the doubts, fears, stress, and anxiety start to creep in, you can refocus on your why and *do the work*.

I've created a process for when doubt, fear, stress, and anxiety creep into my world. I acknowledge it, because, after all, I am a human being and these are completely natural emotions. Then I smile and am grateful for it.

Why? Because I know my competition is experiencing the same emotions at that very moment, and most are letting it get the better of them. My competition is not doing the work because they are letting doubt, fear, stress, and anxiety win.

So, I smile, embrace the doubt, hug the fear, acknowledge the stress, and accept the anxiety. Then I think of my why, rise above it, and create. *The higher the obstacle, the lower the competition.*

Doubt, fear, stress, and anxiety are massive obstacles, so if you join me in embracing these emotions and rising above them, you are truly on the common path to uncommon success!

How I Produce Content

When I first began my entrepreneurial journey, my content production was all over the map. I didn't have a plan. I wasn't productive. I wasn't disciplined. I wasn't focused. I wasn't on the common path to uncommon success.

Thankfully, I figured out how to right the ship, but it took time and it wasn't easy.

There was a lot of trial and error, a lot of coaching from my mentor, a lot of guidance from my mastermind, and lot of learning from the guests I had on *Entrepreneurs on Fire*.

Over time, I developed a system. With this system, I became more productive. With this system, I became more disciplined. With this system, I became more focused.

Every day, I improved some aspect of my system. Over time, *Entrepreneurs on Fire* became a well-oiled machine. We created content at a rapid and efficient rate and were clicking on all cylinders.

I realized the system was successful because I had mastered three things: my productivity, my discipline, and my focus. I decided to identify why these three traits were so important and how I could continue improving in each area.

Productivity

Most people think they're productive. Spoiler alert . . . they're not. They're busy. Being busy is not being productive.

We all have things we need to do every day that aren't bringing us closer to financial freedom and fulfillment, and that's okay. However, those on the common path to uncommon success make sure that time is set aside every day to be productive in the *right* areas.

My definition of productivity: producing the *right* content for your avatar.

Being busy and being productive are two completely different things. But that's how many people live their lives. Always going a million miles an hour, always being busy, thinking they are being productive, but never getting closer to their goals and aspirations because they are never being productive in the true sense of the word.

You are on the common path to uncommon success. You will be productive in the true sense of the word. You will produce the right content. You will achieve financial freedom and fulfillment.

When I figured out what being productive meant, I identified the best use of my "producing time." I was the host of *Entrepreneurs on Fire*. I interviewed successful and inspiring entrepreneurs. Producing the right content meant creating the best podcast interviews I was capable of. Anything else was a distraction.

Anything else was just "being busy."

Discipline

The next step I needed to implement into my life was discipline. A quote I learned as an officer in the US Army was, "No plan survives first contact with the enemy," from Helmuth von Moltke. Those words define the lives of most entrepreneurs. We go to bed at night with the best of intentions.

We intend to awake on the morrow full of zest and vigor, ready to tackle our massive to-do list and conquer the world. Then, we awake and all hell breaks loose. The kids are screaming, the dog is pooping, the doorbell is ringing, the phone is beeping. Our morning is officially derailed, which leads to a derailed afternoon, which causes us to give up in the evening with the promise of *carpe diem!* the following day.

This cycle will repeat until financial freedom and fulfillment seem like a distant dream. I experienced this cycle firsthand and knew I needed stop circling the drain. In that moment, I committed to becoming disciplined.

I define discipline as follows: being a disciple to a plan of action. No longer was I going to awake in the morning with "the best of intentions." I committed to awaking in the morning with a plan of action already in place. I committed to creating my plan the night before. I called this commitment "winning tomorrow today."

I knew if I let my sleepy, hazy, "just woke up" brain take charge, I would not accomplish meaningful tasks. But if I had a rock-solid plan in place that I had created the day prior, there would be nothing to do except execute. My commitment would be staring me in the face and all I had to do was follow the plan.

That one simple tactic of writing down my plan the day before changed everything. Now I awoke with a purpose. There was no procrastination. There was no dedicating brain power to figure out what I should do today. It was all there in black in white.

I became a disciple to the plan of action I created for myself. I became disciplined.

A lot of people like to point to my time in the Army as the reason I am so disciplined. That's so they can feel better about their lack of discipline. Like all human beings, I struggle with distractions. However, by implementing the above discipline of winning tomorrow today, I curbed my distractions, suffocated my procrastinations, and started working on what mattered.

Focus

If you've listened to a few episodes of *Entrepreneurs on Fire*, you know *focus* is my single favorite word. I love it because of what the word stands for, but also because of how easily it turns into an amazing acronym:

Follow One Course Until Success.

I believe this concept is the single biggest reason I built a multi-million-dollar business empire. This one word allowed me to do what no one was willing to attempt. With focus, I created a daily podcast interviewing the world's most inspiring and successful entrepreneurs. I created something new, different, unique, and challenging.

Let me take you back to May 6, 1954. On that day, Roger Bannister did the impossible. He broke the four-minute mile with a time of 3:59.40.

Up to that point, many believed it was scientifically impossible for a human to run a sub-four-minute mile. Roger focused on nothing else and shattered this falsely held belief. Suddenly, others believed it was possible, and over the next five years, twenty-one people ran a sub-four-minute mile.

Coincidence? I think not.

Since the launch of *Entrepreneurs on Fire*, many people have launched daily interview podcasts, some with great levels of success.

Before I shattered the falsely held belief that a daily interview podcast couldn't be successful, the top podcasters in the industry said it couldn't be done. I focused on nothing else besides finding a way to make it happen. Nothing else mattered. Nothing could distract me. I followed one course until I achieved success.

I eventually diversified *Entrepreneurs on Fire*, but only after solidifying my initial focus.

A major struggle of entrepreneurs who are just starting out is a scattered focus. They have all these amazing ideas and give a little bit of time, energy, and effort to each one.

They go one mile wide and one inch deep with their myriad of ideas. Then, they are shocked when their one-inch impressions don't gain any traction or create any impact. Those on the common path to uncommon success go one inch wide and one mile deep.

We *focus* on one thing, go deep, and serve our niche better than anyone else is willing or able to do. If you are not serving your niche better than your competition, you are not niche enough.

From the day *Entrepreneurs on Fire* launched, it was:

The best daily podcast interviewing successful entrepreneurs.

It was . . .

The worst daily podcast interviewing successful entrepreneurs.

It was . . .

The *only* daily podcast interviewing successful entrepreneurs.

See what I did there? *Entrepreneurs on Fire* was the only game in town. If you wanted a podcast that delivered a fresh episode with an inspiring entrepreneur seven days a week, *Entrepreneurs on Fire* was your show.

This was important for several reasons. First off, I knew I was not going to be a good podcast host when I launched. How could I? I had never podcast before. I needed time to hone my skills and put in the reps. Doing a daily podcast would allow me to put in the reps quickly, but I still needed my audience to be patient while I improved my skill set. Being the only show in town ensured they had no choice but to be patient.

Had I tried to launch a weekly podcast while writing my first book and launching my first course, I would have failed at everything. Instead, I focused on one thing. I filled a void in the marketplace and gained traction for *Entrepreneurs on Fire* one listener at a time.

Years later, this level of focus led to an *a-ha* moment. It was 2016. *Entrepreneurs on Fire* had been going strong for four years. We were generating seven figures of revenue a year and were clicking on all cylinders.

As our business evolved, I continued to hone our systems, but it became obvious our success was stemming from those three magical words, productivity, discipline, and focus.

With those three words leading the way, *Entrepreneurs on Fire* was unstoppable. Success leaves clues, and thousands of people were searching for the clues to *Entrepreneurs on Fire*'s success. I decided it was time to reveal the treasure map.

I felt confident that my process would work for any entrepreneur who applied these three simple principles to their business.

Over the next three months, I created the *Mastery Journal*, so people could master productivity, discipline, and focus in a hundred days. Up until this book, the *Mastery Journal* was my best work ever. We launched it on Kickstarter and it was obvious my audience needed this solution. During the thirty-three-day launch, the $39 *Mastery Journal* generated over $280,000 in sales. (If you want to learn more about the *Mastery Journal*, visit TheMasteryJournal.com.)

An Entrepreneur on Fire's Path to Uncommon Success

PAT FLYNN ON CREATING CONTENT

**When creating content,
be the best answer on the internet.**
—ANDY CRESTODINA

IT WAS 2008. Pat, a few years into his architecture career, had recently finished the LEED architecture exam. While preparing for the exam, Pat had been shocked at how little information there had been online regarding the exam except from the company that administered the exam itself.

Pat had created a fantastic study guide after passing the exam and decided to turn it into an e-book to sell online. That decision eventually netted Pat more than $200,000. Desperate test-takers flocked to his e-book and happily paid the quoted price, knowing a passing grade on this exam was critical for their career.

Laid off after taking the exam, Pat knew he had one of two options. He could join the thousands of other laid-off architects and get in line for the next job opening, or he could dedicate himself to promoting his guide and building a website. Lucky for us, Pat chose option two and later launched a blog called SmartPassiveIncome.com.

Through trial and error, Pat developed a formula he now uses on every piece of content he creates so he can reach more people, teach more people, and make a bigger impact. Pat's formula:

1. **Start with the end in mind and reverse engineer the transformation.** What is the transformation you are looking to provide to your audience? What is the purpose of the content? What is your goal, your north star?

2. **Use stories, step-by-step guides, case studies, and quotes to support the transformation.**

3. **Do a complete brain dump of all your ideas.** The brain does a great job at coming up with ideas but a terrible job at organizing them.

4. **Organize the ideas into an order and hierarchy.** Organize the ideas from where you need to start all the way through the transformation.

5. **Create the hook.** What is going to draw your audience in? What will make them stick around? What loop can you open that the content will close?

6. **Create the title.** Make sure to be clear, concise, and use keywords so your content will rank well with SEO (search engine optimization).

After following the above steps, Pat is ready to create his post, podcast, video, or all three! In Pat's own words: "Your earnings are a direct by-product of how well you serve your audience. Put yourself in their shoes and provide solutions to their struggles. If you can provide your audience with small wins, you'll be given the opportunity to provide bigger wins, which will result in more success for you and your business."

Thank you, Pat Flynn.

You can learn more about Pat at SmartPassiveIncome.com.

Check out your free companion course for added support along *The Common Path to Uncommon Success*: EOFire.com/success-course.

CHAPTER 9

Launch

The most dangerous way we sabotage ourselves is by waiting for the perfect moment to begin. Nothing works perfectly the first time, or the first fifty times. Everything has a learning curve. The beginning is just that—a beginning. Surrender your desire to do it flawlessly on the first try. It's not possible. Learn to learn. Learn to fail. Learn to learn from failing.
—VIRONIKA TUGALEVA

Perfectionism. It's a curse. I'm sure you've uttered words along the lines of, "I just wish I wasn't such a perfectionist." Yuck. We've all done it.

There's no shame in giving yourself what you think is a backhanded compliment. The shame is continuing to do so. Perfectionism sucks. Perfectionism is a word you hide behind so you never have to face the possibility of rejection, failure, or fear.

Let those who will never taste uncommon success live in their fairy tale of perfectionism. Let them cower behind that word and use it as an excuse to hide from the world. In the years to come, they'll regret their lack of action when they realize how little they accomplished over their lifetime.

You won't. You will imperfectly, awkwardly, and clumsily launch your voice, message, and mission into the world. On your path to uncommon success.

You'll stumble, you'll fall, you'll struggle. You'll learn to learn, learn to fail, learn to learn from failing. The best part? You'll survive.

This process will repeat over and over and then one magical day something will click and your life will never be the same. You'll see uncommon success forming right before your eyes and all the hardship and struggle you endured up to that point will fade into a distant memory of satisfaction and dedication.

> First they ignore you, then they laugh at you,
> then they fight you, then you win.
> —MAHATMA GANDHI

But none of this can happen until you *launch*. Up until this point, I've been guiding and preparing you for this very moment. Now it's up to you.

The red button is in your hands. Go ahead. Press it. It's time. It's time to launch.

My Launch Story

Some of this you've already heard, but I think it's important here. It was August 14, 2012. I had been working with my mentor for two months. I had forty interviews completed and scheduled for release. My website was up, my social media accounts were active, and my email opt-in form was functioning properly.

Tomorrow was the big day. The day I had been building up to for months. *Entrepreneurs on Fire* was going to launch and my idea was going to become reality.

> If you are not embarrassed by the first version
> of your product, you've launched too late.
> —REID HOFFMAN

I didn't sleep much that night. I tossed, turned, and had a few nerve-racking dreams of my launch. At 4:30 a.m., I awoke with a start, the hands of terror firmly grasped around my neck.

I was not ready.

Entrepreneurs on Fire was not ready.

I had to stop this. I had to stop this *now!*

I jumped out of bed, rushed over to my computer, and in a flurry of keystrokes canceled everything that was scheduled to launch my podcast in mere hours. I then composed a quick email to my mentor, explaining why I had to push back my launch a couple weeks. As soon as I pressed *send,* I knew it was a load of BS, but fear was guiding my every move.

With the launch officially delayed, I sat down with a relieved sigh. I thought to myself, *I just dodged a bullet! My website is not perfect, my social media is not perfect, my email opt-in is not perfect, and now I have two weeks to make everything perfect.*

As I type these words today, they seem so silly. I didn't know the common path to uncommon success was full of imperfection.

My initial two-week delay became three. Three weeks became four. Four weeks became five. I was cowering behind the wall of perfectionism and it was jeopardizing everything I had worked so hard for.

Finally, my mentor stepped in and wrote the words that saved *Entrepreneurs on Fire.*

John, I know what you're doing and I know why, because I've been there too. It's scary to put your art out into the world, especially when you know it's not that good. But you must. In fact, here's an ultimatum. If you don't launch this week, I will fire you as a mentee.

Those words rocked my world. The only thing I feared more than launching was losing the guidance of my mentor. So, on September 21, 2012, I launched *Entrepreneurs on Fire* and put my very imperfect art out into the world.

Looking back, I know exactly why I was overcome with dread on launch day. I was living in a pre-launch fantasy. Before you launch, anything is possible. Success beyond our wildest dreams is possible. Failure below our worst nightmare is possible. Anything in the middle of those two extremes is possible.

I knew *Entrepreneurs on Fire* was a good idea. I knew it *might* work. I also knew it might not work.

If I stayed in my pre-launch fantasy, I could keep hoping for the best and brightest future. But once that *launch* button was pushed, the fantasy bubble would pop and reality would set in. Reality might contain a happy ending, but it also contained bad ones. Why not just live in my cozy bubble of "what if" a little longer? Why not delay that possible pain if *Entrepreneurs on Fire* just didn't work?

These thoughts happened at a subconscious level. I didn't even realize I was thinking this way until I took the time to reflect post-launch. I've seen countless entrepreneurs get stuck in the same pre-launch fantasy I was stuck in. My mentor empathically popped my fairy-tale bubble, but not everyone is so lucky.

I've seen entrepreneurs with amazing art to share with the world falter at the starting gate, consumed with perfection. They never launch and inevitably fade away into nothingness, consumed by their fear, doubt, and "what if." Their art is never shared with the world and their message impacts no one.

You are on the common path to uncommon success. We launch. We launch ugly, we launch awkwardly, we launch scared. But the important thing is, we launch.

You got this!

An Entrepreneur on Fire's Path to Uncommon Success

JEFF WALKER ON LAUNCH

The way to get started is to quit talking and begin doing.
—WALT DISNEY

WHEN I ASKED JEFF to contribute to this chapter, he said with a smile: *Sure, I can fit twenty-five years of experience into one chapter.* We'll do our best.

Jeff started out as a stay-at-home dad. His first launch was in 1996. He had been publishing a free newsletter on the stock market for quite some time and decided it was time to get paid!

There was one major problem. Jeff had no marketing or sales experience. On top of that, Jeff felt uncomfortable asking for the sale—he wasn't a natural salesman. To combat these deficiencies, Jeff committed to providing so much value to his audience that when he finally made the offer, they wouldn't be able to say no.

Over the next few weeks, Jeff delivered on that promise. He delivered incredibly detailed stock market reports with massive amounts of value. He built up his goodwill to a fever pitch and then asked for the order.

A week later, Jeff had made $1,650. For Jeff, this was life-changing money and put him in business. It proved that people would buy from him. It also proved that people would buy from those who were delivering value online.

Remember, this was 1996.

That was Jeff's *a-ha* moment. He did this successfully once, why couldn't he do it again and again and again? An added benefit? He might even get better!

Jeff's next launch did $6,000. His third, $8,000. Fast-forward a couple years and Jeff did a $34,000 launch.

The sky was the limit. Jeff and his growing family found their dream home in the mountains of Colorado, but they needed a down payment. This need inspired a launch that put Jeff on the map.

He created his best offer to date, built massive anticipation, and completed a launch that generated $106,000 in seven days. This simply blew Jeff's mind. During his previous life in corporate, Jeff had never made more than $35,000 in a year. He had just made $106,000 in a week.

Wow.

At this point you may be wondering . . . what exactly is a launch? Let's talk Hollywood. When the movie studios roll out a new movie, they don't just appear one day. There's a buildup. They create trailers and send their actors to talk shows to build up as much publicity as possible before the movie premier.

You want to do the same. You want people to be anticipating your offer *before* it's available. You want to create buzz.

In 2005, Jeff released the course *Product Launch Formula* to help others learn how to successfully launch their products and services. Every year, Jeff and his team publish an updated version. Over the past fifteen-plus years, people have used *Product Launch Formula* in every location, niche, and language you can imagine.

Jeff published the book *Launch*, which instantly became a *New York Times* #1 bestseller.

When it comes to launching, Jeff is the acknowledged leader and loves sharing the wisdom he's gained over the years with those who are seeking success with their launches.

Here are a few key takeaways from Jeff about launching.

1. Launching gives you position in the market as the go-to resource.
2. There are limitless businesses that people can give their money to. If you want to be the person they choose, you must stand out.

3. Hope marketing is when you create the product and hope someone buys from you.

4. Hope marketing never works.

5. An engineered, structured launch will give you the momentum you need to build your following and ensure you have sales on day one.

6. Sales are like oxygen for your business because they allow you to build your team, increase your marketing, and improve your product or service.

7. Sales put you in business and keep you in business.

8. Put one step in front of another, keep launching, learn from your mistakes, and get better each time.

Jeff has now helped generate over a billion dollars in sales with *Product Launch Formula*. In Jeff's own words: "Launching is within your reach. All you need to do is deliver value ahead of time, build anticipation, and have an engineered, structured launch. At the end of the day, you need to launch. You cannot depend on hope marketing."

Thank you, Jeff Walker.

You can learn more about Jeff at JeffWalker.com.

Check out your free companion course for added support along *The Common Path to Uncommon Success*: EOFire.com/success-course.

CHAPTER 10

Pinpoint Your Avatar's Biggest Struggle

Inside of every problem lies an opportunity.
—ROBERT KIYOSAKI

There is a major misconception on the common path to uncommon success that stops most people from even starting: they doubt their ability to identify an idea that will generate revenue for their business. This doubt turns to fear, this fear becomes paralyzing, and everything stops.

This won't happen to you. Why? You are on the common path, and this path is straightforward and clear.

You've identified your big idea. You've niched down into an underserved market. You've created your avatar and chosen your platform. You have your mentor and have joined (or formed) a mastermind.

Now, you're simply going to take the next step. That step? Pinpointing your avatar's biggest struggle.

Following the guidance of the common path to uncommon success, you're producing free, valuable, and consistent content on a platform of your choice. Maybe it's podcasting, vlogging, blogging, social media, some other platform you've chosen, or a combination of the above. By producing free, valuable, and consistent content for your avatar, you are naturally growing an audience.

That audience is beginning to know, like, and trust you because of the value you are adding to their lives. Now, it's time to engage with your audience and ask them four simple questions.

1. How did you hear about me/find my content?
2. What do you like about the content I'm producing?
3. What don't you like?
4. What is your biggest struggle right now?

You may be wondering, "How do I engage with this audience I am building?" Don't overcomplicate things. If you've been building an email list, send them an email. If you're connected with them on social media, send them a private message.

Whatever platforms you are using to produce content, use those same platforms to pose these questions.

It just needs to be a simple message like:

Hi [name],

Thank you for listening to/watching my content. I'd love to jump on a quick call to ask you four questions. It would really help me to learn more about you.
    Thanks!

—John

The key is to engage with as many people in your audience as possible, one-on-one.

Yes, I said one-on-one. I know a lot of people only believe in doing things at scale. You'll hear them say, "Speaking to people one-on-one is trading time for money and I want to grow a business where I can leverage my time and knowledge."

Those people never achieve uncommon success. You will get to a place where you're leveraging your time and knowledge, but you're not there yet. At this stage on the common path, you need to do things that don't scale. You need to ask the people who are consuming your content these four questions, and you must do it one-on-one. It's the only way you will get the honest and detailed responses you need.

Why these four specific questions? Let me break them down.

How did you hear about me/find my content?

This question is critical because it will reveal how people are finding you and your content. Once you collect several responses to this question, you'll be able to pour igniter fluid on the ways your avatars are finding you. Just as important: you'll be able to stop wasting your time in areas that aren't.

Maybe a lot of your avatars are telling you about a guest post they read on someone's website. You now know you need to find a way to work with that person on more projects.

Maybe none of your avatars mention the Facebook ads you've been running and you can save that time and money by stopping that lead acquisition strategy that is not producing your best leads.

Your best leads are those who will jump on a five-minute call with you to answer these four questions, so treat them like the gold they are.

What do you like about the content I am producing?

This question is critical because, until we ask, we never truly know what is resonating with our avatars. Plus, they will love that they are being heard. When you start to see trends on specific topics, it's time to double down on this type of content and keep up the heat!

What don't you like about the content I am producing?

This question will ensure you are not making a simple mistake with your content that could be easily corrected. An error many people make when they start getting responses to this question is to change things immediately.

Never adjust what you are doing based off of one response. That person could just be an anomaly and giving you bad feedback. You need to see a trend of multiple people not liking the same thing about your content before you implement a change.

What is your biggest struggle right now?

This is far and away the most important question you will ask. The answers you receive will dictate the next step you take. You need to document *every* response to this question and sort the responses based on similarity. You will see trends develop.

My recommendation is to get at least thirty responses to this question and look for groups of at least five similar struggles.

Now it's your turn to identify which struggle you want to create the solution for. Don't overcomplicate things. You need to have a bias for action and a disgust for perfection.

Our goal is to offer real solutions to our avatar's real problems. Choose the struggle you are going to create the solution for. Follow your intuition.

Your first offer may not work, nor your second, but if you keep at this process long enough you'll identify an irresistible offer that your audience is willing to invest their hard-earned money in.

Once you've identified the struggle you are going to tackle first, it's time to laser focus on creating the perfect solution, which we'll be covering in the next chapter.

My Avatar's Biggest Struggle

Problems are not stop signs, they are guidelines.
—ROBERT H. SCHULLER

It was August of 2013. *Entrepreneurs on Fire* had been rocking for eleven months. I had published over 330 episodes. I had hit many of my goals, such as connecting with amazing entrepreneurs as guests of my show, growing my audience and influence, providing free, valuable, and consistent content—all while managing to generate a trickle of revenue through sponsorships and coaching.

However, it was time to turn that trickle of revenue into a waterfall. It was time to take things to the next level financially. How? The first step was identifying my avatar's biggest struggle.

Most people approach this problem from the wrong direction. They think they must lock themselves in a cold, dark room and not exit until they've come up with the biggest problem their avatars are facing. The problem with this line of thought is that your avatar is no longer just words on a page.

You've been creating free, valuable, and consistent content for some time now. Your avatar is a real person. Your avatar is the audience you've grown while providing value, and they know, like, and trust you.

Now it's time to ask them, "What is your biggest struggle right now?"

In August of 2013, these were the exact questions I asked my audience, whom I lovingly referred to as Fire Nation.

I sent out emails, I created a specific podcast episode requesting direct feedback on this very question, I made social media posts, and sent private messages via this platform, all with the same question, "What is your biggest struggle right now?"

The responses started pouring in. I painstakingly documented and categorized each response, and was fascinated with the answers. In one week, I learned more about Fire Nation than I had in the previous eleven months.

I learned about their hopes, their fears, their dreams, and their doubts. It shaped the type of content I produced for years to come. But most importantly it provided the answer I was looking for. "What is your biggest struggle right now?"

Out of all the responses, one theme rose to the top.

John, I love how you've created a platform to share your voice, message, and mission with the world. My passion is [gardening, fitness, music, etc.] and I'd love to be able to create a podcast platform to share my passion and knowledge with the world and become an authority figure and influencer in this niche, but I don't know the first thing about starting a podcast. Can you help me create and launch my podcast, then show me how to grow and monetize this platform?

Frankly, I was a little stunned. It had never occurred to me that, even though I was less than a year in, people would look at me as "expert enough" to coach them in the creation of their own podcast. Also, I had no idea there was such an appetite out there for people to create their own podcasts. I thought I was one of the lone weirdos that wanted to host their own show, but boy was I wrong.

So there it was. I had asked, and Fire Nation had answered in no uncertain terms. It was time for me to create the solution, which is what the next chapter is focused on.

Spoiler alert: my first attempt at creating the "solution" was a *big* swing and a miss.

I eventually got it right, but as much as I hope you emulate my successes, I hope you avoid my failures, and there are plenty of those to go around, believe you me.

It's time for the next stage along our common path to uncommon success. Create the solution to your avatar's biggest struggle.

Let's go!

An Entrepreneur on Fire's Path to Uncommon Success

RYAN LEVESQUE ON PINPOINTING YOUR AVATAR'S BIGGEST STRUGGLE

To make our communications more effective, we need to shift our thinking from "What information do I need to convey?" to "What questions do I want my audience to ask?"
—CHIP HEATH

SCRABBLE TILE JEWELRY? Ryan looked in the mirror and wondered how his life had led him to this point.

He was an Ivy League graduate. He was motivated, ambitious, and intelligent. Yet here he was trying to teach people how to create Scrabble tile jewelry online. Life had certainly taken some interesting twists and turns.

It was time for a walk. Ryan needed to clear his head and give himself time to think.

As he strolled along a crowded sidewalk, Ryan thought about the other obscure niches he had conquered over the years: orchid care, satellite TV, water filtration systems, memory improvement—and, of course, Scrabble tile jewelry.

How had he done it? What was the common denominator of success? He had *asked* the right questions to the right people.

It was really that simple. In that very moment, Ryan committed to turning that simple concept into a methodology that he could use to help other business owners grow and scale their businesses as he had his.

Ryan had his big idea and it no longer involved Scrabble tile jewelry.

Fast-forward a couple years and Ryan's big idea was a three-time Inc. 5000 company that has helped thousands of business owners scale their business by knowing the right questions to ask.

But wait a second . . .

Didn't Henry Ford say: *If I asked people what they wanted, they would have asked for faster horses?*

Didn't Steve Jobs say: *People don't know what they want until I show it to them?*

Yes, they did. People don't know what they want till you show them what they want. To discover what your avatar wants, you must go through the side door. That side door will open when you ask these three questions.

1. **S.M.I.Q: The single most important question: When it comes to X, what is the single biggest challenge or frustration you are dealing with right now? Please be as detailed and specific as possible.** Always pay close attention to the specific language your avatar uses. This is the language you will be using in your marketing efforts going forward. Always look for the detailed responses, for these are your buyers. An example: When it comes to orchid care, what is the single biggest challenge or frustration you are dealing with right now? Please be as detailed and specific as possible. You are looking for detailed answers such as, "I'm struggling with replanting my orchid—it always dies no matter what I do." That is a real pain point. If you can create the solution for that, you'll have a buyer.

2. **If you were to quantify it, how much time have you invested trying to solve this problem?** You are looking for people who have experienced a lot of pain and have spent a lot of time trying to solve this problem. These are the people who would pay for the right solution right now.

3. **How much money have you invested trying to solve this specific challenge?** Past behavior is the best predictor of future behavior. If people have spent money in the past, they are more likely to invest money in the future.

Ryan's book *Ask* is an international bestseller with hundreds of thousands of copies sold. Make sure to pick up a copy to further your knowledge on this topic. In Ryan's own words: "These three questions will help you pinpoint the hyper-responsive segment of your market and the specific language they use to describe that problem so you can echo it back in your marketing and in your product."

Thank you, Ryan Levesque.

You can learn more about Ryan at AskMethod.com.

Check out your free companion course for added support along *The Common Path to Uncommon Success*: EOFire.com/success-course.

CHAPTER 11

Prove the Concept and Craft the Solution

*Approach each customer with the idea of
helping him or her solve a problem or achieve
a goal, not of selling a product or service.*
—BRIAN TRACY

You've done all the right things along your common path to uncommon success. You've delivered free, valuable, and consistent
content to your avatar. You now have an audience that knows, likes,
and trusts you. You've asked that audience what their biggest struggle
is, documenting and categorizing their response. You identified which
struggle you'll create the solution for.

Now it's time to roll up your sleeves and craft the solution, right?
Wrong.

This is where many stray off the path toward uncommon success.
This is where many would lock themselves away for months, crafting
the perfect solution, finally emerging from their cave of isolation to

proudly announce to the world, *"I hath returned bearing the world's greatest solution to your most grave and unjust problem."*

Then they'll hear the following sound: Cricket. Cricket. Cricket.

Don't get me wrong, the above strategy works some of the time because you've done most things right on your common path to uncommon success. But this is a narrow path and there is no need to stray.

Before we craft the perfect solution for our audience, we need to verify that people will pay for the solution. Remember this truism: *People vote with their wallet.*

If you are going to spend your most valuable asset, time, to create the perfect solution to your audience's biggest struggle, you must know with 100 percent certainty that your audience is willing to invest in the solution. I've made the grievous error of not proving my idea before creating, and I heard crickets.

Luckily, I learned my lesson. Now, before I spend the time to craft the solution, I insist that my audience prove the concept by voting with their wallet. If people are not willing to prepay, or at the very least put a deposit down for a solution I am offering to create, their struggle is not painful enough.

I have saved myself hundreds of hours of fruitless effort by sticking to this strategy. In the next section, I will share a personal example of both how I failed and succeeded with this strategy.

But first, let's identify what your solution could be. Your solution will most likely be a product, a service, or a community. Some examples would be the following:

- One-on-one coaching
- Group coaching
- Leading a mastermind
- Writing a book
- Creating a course
- Hosting a virtual summit
- Running a paid challenge
- Creating software (SaaS: Software as a Service)

- Creating a physical product
- Hosting a premium community
- Becoming an affiliate and promoting another company's product, service, or community
- Offering a certification
- Hosting live or virtual events

Below are examples from my personal experience running *Entrepreneurs on Fire*.

One-on-One Coaching

I'll never forget the first revenue I made with *Entrepreneurs on Fire*. A couple of months after I launched, a listener reached out and shared he was launching his podcast soon and having some issues. He had been following my successful launch and was looking for guidance.

I did not yet have a coaching program in place, but his request jolted me into action. On the spot, I created a one-, two-, and three-month coaching program. I still remember the price points: $800 for one month, $1,400 for two, and $1,800 for three. I outlined the coaching would include a weekly thirty-minute call and unlimited email access. I pressed *send*. Minutes later, the response came back that he'd take the three-month program. I was in a small state of shock. I had generated $1,800 in a few minutes based off an email I had just received. Obviously, there was a lot of work to be done, but I was to the moon. Proof of concept for one-on-one coaching had occurred and I was committed to over-delivering to my first student.

Leading a Mastermind

About a year into *Entrepreneurs on Fire*, I was seeing great momentum with both the podcast and the growth of my audience. The daily listens were growing, the engagement level was high, and I was being featured in a lot of media outlets about this little niche called podcasting. I was enjoying my interactions with my audience, Fire Nation, whether it be through email, social media, or even regular old snail mail.

A consistent theme from these communications was that my audience would love a place to interact with other listeners of *Entrepreneurs on Fire*. I realized this was my opportunity to create a mastermind. I reached out to other entrepreneurs who had successfully run paid masterminds and learned their best practices. Soon, I was ready to announce the launch of Fire Nation Elite.

Fire Nation Elite would consist of weekly live calls for open Q&A, a Facebook group for daily interaction, and each month I would host a guest speaker to present on a topic of their expertise. I decided to cap Fire Nation Elite at a hundred members and interview every single applicant before offering them a spot.

Fire Nation Elite was going to be a family for my foreseeable future and I knew that it was critical that we formed a community that was committed to supporting and guiding each other on this difficult journey of entrepreneurship.

We started the price point at $300 per quarter, with a minimum three-month commitment. We increased that price point in the months ahead based on supply and demand and always committed to delivering ten times the value of the membership.

I'll never forget the first live call we had with Fire Nation Elite. It was amazing to see so many amazing and committed people in one place, all eager to learn and support each other. Over the next two-and-a-half years, Fire Nation Elite generated an average of $12,000 a month in revenue. Kate and I poured our heart and soul into Fire Nation Elite and the friendships we formed are still present to this day, while the success stories still make my heart sing.

Writing a Book

Three months into the launch of *Entrepreneurs on Fire*, all was going well. I decided it was time to further my knowledge on podcasting, so I went to Amazon to buy all the books I could find on the topic. To my shock, there was not a single book dedicated to the topic of podcasting.

At that moment in time, I had been immersed in the topic of podcasting for about seven months. I was by no means the #1 podcast expert in the world, but I knew more than 99 percent of people in the world on the topic. To them, I was an expert. I knew a book on podcasting had to be written and I decided to be the person to do so.

The very next day, I created an outline and then proceeded to write the first draft of *Podcast Launch* in about twenty writing hours. When I pressed the publish button to make *Podcast Launch* live in the Amazon bookstore, it was an amazing feeling.

Was it perfect? No. Was it the best book on podcasting in Amazon? Yes. Was it the worst? Yes. It was the *only* book on podcasting in Amazon.

I immediately started seeing the benefit. Sales were rolling in at the rate of ten to twenty a day. I had priced the book at $2.99, so it was never going to be a massive moneymaker, but it was proving to be an incredible lead generator.

Downloads of *Entrepreneurs on Fire* increased noticeably. My email list and social media followings grew substantially. Messages specifically about the book began to stream in. I had delivered real value at a fair price point and people were grateful.

It also increased my credibility. More speaking opportunities arose. After all, I was now the guy who wrote the book on podcasting. Overall, writing *Podcast Launch* increased the awareness and value of my brand exponentially, as well as generated revenue through book sales, grew my email marketing list, and drew more listeners to *Entrepreneurs on Fire*, which increased sponsorship revenue and course sales when I implemented both into my business in the ensuing years.

If you can find a void in the book marketplace for your niche, writing a book is an incredible use of your time and effort.

Creating a Course

In the next section of this chapter, I will share my experience launching Podcasters' Paradise, but in this section I will share a short rundown of my experience launching our course Webinar on Fire.

In 2014, our podcasting course (Podcasters' Paradise) had been going strong for almost a year and we were hosting live webinars every week to promote the course. We were having a ton of success with webinars, and in addition to questions on podcasting we were receiving a lot of questions regarding our webinar system.

When the umpteenth question came through about webinars, I knew it was time to create a course. We launched Webinar on Fire in January of 2014 and it was a perfect addition to Podcasters' Paradise. Webinar on Fire was a great revenue stream for us over the years. It taught us a valuable lesson to always listen to your audience and let their biggest struggles guide you.

Hosting a Virtual Summit

A virtual summit is typically a collection of video interviews from experts focused on a certain topic, delivered to an audience over the course of several days, with an offer at the end. Hosting a virtual summit can be a great way to kick-start many parts of your business. It will make you choose a specific topic, identify the biggest struggles, and deliver the best solutions.

Once you have chosen the topic, you will need to identify authority figures who are willing to present on their topic of expertise. Virtual summits will fast-track your online marketing skills as you'll have to learn how to create landing pages, connect them to your email provider, host videos, and release them upon a prearranged schedule—as well as create and pitch an offer.

These skills are critical to master along your common path to uncommon success, so it's important to do something like this early in your journey as it will take multiple attempts at projects like this to start creating systems and processes that will lead to future success.

Above and beyond everything above, a virtual summit will help build your email list, create connections with authority figures, improve your presentation skills, and force you to learn how to make an offer. Dr. Mark T. Wade at HustleandScale.com is my go-to resource for all things virtual summits.

Running a Paid Challenge

A paid challenge is typically a three-, five-, seven-, ten-, fifteen-, or thirty-day online event that delivers a promised result. An example of a challenge I participated in was "The Ten-Pound Takedown by Cristy 'Code Red' Nickel." The goal of the challenge was to lose ten pounds in thirty days. Every day for a month, Cristy sent an email with the marching orders for that day as well as an inspirational video to keep us motivated. We also had access to a Facebook group where everyone else taking part in the challenge was there to support and guide each other over these thirty days.

When you have your sights set on one goal and are pursuing that goal with supportive and like-minded individuals, your likelihood of success skyrockets. The challenge was $47, and throughout the challenge there were multiple upsells for Cristy's private coaching, which is where the real profit margin was.

I've hosted a few challenges myself. One was in preparation for the launch of Tony Robbins's course called Knowledge Broker Blueprint. As affiliates, I knew we needed to warm up our audience for launch day, so Kate and I partnered up with Jill and Josh Stanton of *Screw the Nine to Five* and created a five-day "Think Like an Expert" challenge.

Over the course of the five-day challenge, we delivered daily live trainings with specific calls to action each day. We also hosted a very active Facebook group where we would answer questions and address struggles daily. When the launch day arrived, we hosted a watch party to build excitement for the offer. We generated over $500,000 in sales for Tony's course and out of over five thousand affiliates we came in fifth place, earning a trip to Fiji to spend four days with Tony at his private resort, Namale.

When we analyzed our sales, we found that the clear majority came from those who participated in the five-day challenge. We had fostered a family environment that was brimming with trust. When we told our challenge participants that we believed in Tony's course and thought they should invest, many did—and we are still hearing success stories from those who took that leap to this very day.

In conclusion, a paid challenge can be a great way to deliver massive value to a group of like-minded people, as well as deliver an incredible result that will develop a high level of trust. Typically, paid challenges range from $7 to $97 and last anywhere between five and thirty days. Free challenges are worth testing when you are just starting out, but once you get your systems and offer down you'll want to work with people who have skin in the game and have invested in the challenge. When people pay, they pay attention.

Creating a Software Service

I don't have any direct experience in the SaaS (Software as a Service) area, but I will share with you what I have seen and learned over the years. SaaS has pros and cons.

Let's talk about the pros first. If you get it right, you can scale and leverage very fast. Slack is a great example of a company that created a piece of software for their internal team, and once they recognized it was better than anything in the marketplace, they decided to pivot their focus to scaling and selling Slack.

Another pro is reliable monthly recurring revenue. When you have a certain number of people paying every month for a service, you can forecast your revenue with extreme accuracy and plan your future accordingly.

A con of SaaS is the up-front cost of investing in the infrastructure and team needed to get the software out to market. There is no guarantee the service will gain traction, and you may not be able to recoup your initial investment.

We partnered with a company in 2014 to build a SaaS offer. They had the team in place, a really good idea, and the desire to scale. But even with our sizable audience we were unable to get the initial traction to keep the project going. Looking back, we weren't offering a solution to a big enough pain point.

Overall, I think SaaS is an advanced business model that should not be attempted early in the entrepreneurial journey,

Creating a Physical Product

I consider a physical product anything you can touch or hold with your hands. I stayed away from physical products over the first three years of *Entrepreneurs on Fire* and focused on virtual offerings. Podcasters' Paradise was a success, Webinar on Fire was rocking and rolling, sponsorship dollars were rolling in, and we were generating significant revenue from affiliate partnerships.

It was time to add another revenue stream, so I asked my audience what their biggest struggle was. The overwhelming response was their struggle setting and accomplishing goals. On *Entrepreneurs on Fire,* my guests shared the importance of goal-setting. My listeners took notice and requested a step-by-step process where they could set and accomplish their goals in a specific time frame.

When I sat down to plan the creation of this step-by-step process, I knew it would have to be something you could hold in your hands. I sketched out the concept of a faux-leather journal, and it felt right. I went into research mode and learned everything I could about setting and accomplishing goals. The result was the *Freedom Journal,* a step-by-step guide to setting and accomplishing your #1 goal in a hundred days. Once the concept was complete, I partnered with a company called Prouduct.com, founded by my friend Richie Norton. Prouduct took the concept and created the physical version.

When I held the finished product in my hands, I knew the *Freedom Journal* was something special. I knew it represented a real solution to my audience's problem.

My next step was to decide how to reveal this product to the world. After a lot of deliberation, I decided to use a crowdfunding platform called Kickstarter. Crowdfunding platforms are great as they allow you to prove the concept of your idea before you go all in.

I printed a few *Freedom Journals* for the launch, but I was waiting to place my big order based off the Kickstarter results. I was going to prove the concept of the *Freedom Journal* before going all in.

I held a thirty-three-day campaign and poured all my marketing efforts into it. Within twenty-five-minutes I had reached my initial goal of $25,000, and by the end of day one had crossed $100,000 of revenue. By the end of the campaign, the *Freedom Journal* became the sixth-most funded publishing campaign of all time, generating $453,810.

The *Freedom Journal* has now gone on to cross the million-dollar mark in sales and I have launched two other journals, the *Mastery Journal* and the *Podcast Journal.* (Please check them out at TheFreedomJournal .com, TheMasteryJournal.com, and ThePodcastJournal.com.)

I believe physical products can be a powerful differentiator in the right scenarios, but you must know your profit margins and understand the cost of storing and shipping inventory. Otherwise, you could be doing a lot of work for what turns out to be very little net profit at the end of the day.

Hosting a Premium Community

A premium community is typically a group of people who are paying a monthly fee to be a part of a group of individuals that are looking to further their knowledge and increase their revenue around a certain topic or industry. We've been running a premium community called Podcasters' Paradise here at *Entrepreneurs on Fire* since 2013. I won't go into too much detail now as I share the full story in the following section, but what typically sets a premium community apart from a mastermind are the video tutorials, templates, and structured guides to help the community members become experts in the topic of focus.

This opportunity once again illustrates the power of niching down into an underserved market, becoming the expert, and creating the tools needed for others to increase their knowledge and competence.

Becoming an Affiliate for a Product or Service

Becoming an affiliate to promote another company's products or services is a great way to generate revenue, especially in the early stages of your journey. When you become an affiliate, you are recommending a company's products or services in return for a percentage of the sale. The percentage will vary based on several factors, but this is a great way for you to find products and services that you know, like, and trust to recommend to your audience.

A great way to get your audience excited about the products and services you are promoting is to write reviews, create video tutorials on how to use the product, interview the founder, and advertise. We have been generating significant revenue as affiliates for years at *Entrepreneurs on Fire*. Our biggest and most significant affiliate revenue comes from our partnership with ClickFunnels.

ClickFunnels is a company we have used in our business for years to create funnels, landing pages, sales pages, one-click upsells, and so much more. I'm good friends with the founder, Russell Brunson, and have had him as a guest on *Entrepreneurs on Fire* many times.

I know many people in my audience would benefit from using a valuable service such as ClickFunnels, so we happily promote them when the opportunity arises. As a result, we've generated over $1.3 million in commissions to date.

My advice to you is to make a list of the products and services you find yourself using often. Go to each company's website, scroll all the way to the bottom, and typically in the footer you will see a link for affiliates. On that page, they will share the specifics of their affiliate program and how you can sign up. If you don't find the affiliate link easily, simply use their contact form and ask to be connected with their affiliate manager.

Affiliate revenue can be a great revenue stream when done correctly. Start by following the steps I shared above and share your affiliate link with your audience where and when it makes sense.

The last piece of advice I will share here is this: you must believe in the products and services you are promoting. Always do what is best for your audience and you will remain firmly on the common path to uncommon success.

Offering a Certification

Credibility is very important. I wouldn't want a surgeon to operate on me who hasn't been to med school. I wouldn't want an architect to design my house who hasn't graduated from an architecture school. Most people want to see some sort of certification showing where you have acquired the knowledge you are claiming to have.

This is where a certification comes in. Once you've become an expert in your industry and are achieving a certain level of success, people will want to learn from you. It happened to me with podcasting, and the result was Podcasters' Paradise. Besides creating a course, you can explore the option of creating a certification. Once an individual went through your certification program, they would then be certified to perform the activity your certification provides.

It's important to remember that your reputation is on the line, so you want to ensure that everyone who becomes certified through your program is worthy and ready to provide the services required. A certification program done right can be a great revenue generator as you typically have an up-front fee for the program as well as a recurring fee on an annual basis to remain certified. Of course, this will mean you will have to keep the certification program fully updated.

I typically see certifications being used successfully in the health and wellness field, although they can be used effectively in other industries as well.

Hosting Live or Virtual Events

These are either in-person or online events where you are delivering value on a predetermined topic, typically over a one-, two-, or three-day period.

I'll start with in-person events. Although these can be a lot of work coordinating travel and accommodation, the incredible energy and experience an in-person event delivers is hard to beat. Kate and I have hosted one-, two-, and three-day events over the years and are always blown away at how much we enjoy them. There's just something special about bringing together people from around the world who are there to learn from and support each other. Hosting a live event is a lot of work on many levels, but in my experience, there is no better way to make a bigger impact in people's lives than with an in-person live event.

We hosted forty people for a three-day event and it was simply incredible to witness the breakthroughs and connections that were made in such a short time. If you're looking to make a massive impact on your tribe, host a live event. You won't regret it.

Virtual events can also be very powerful when done right. They have a lot of similarities to virtual summits so I won't go into much detail here, but the key thing to remember is this: You know your avatar. You know your audience. Create the event *they* would want. Fortune favors the bold, so step up in your boldness and create magic.

In Conclusion

The above are several ways you'll be able to generate revenue through solutions you're providing to your audience's biggest struggles. Don't be overwhelmed with all the options—simply remember the best course of action is to ask your audience to share their biggest struggle, identify the solution you want to deliver, get proof of concept, then craft and deliver the solution.

You got this!

My Solution

In the previous chapter, I shared the process of how I identified my audience's biggest struggle. I'm going to recap and expound upon that now, followed by a solution I created and failed miserably with, and one I knocked out of the park.

> For every problem, there is a solution
> which is simple, clean, and wrong.
> —H. L. MENCKEN

Entrepreneurs on Fire was *en fuego*. It was August of 2013 and I had released 330 episodes over eleven months. Downloads were increasing month over month and my confidence was growing with each interview I published. Everything was going as planned.

Everything except one thing: revenue. As my one-year anniversary of launching *Entrepreneurs on Fire* approached, I looked at my numbers and saw I was going to make less than $28,000 for the year. Not terrible, but not a number I wanted to repeat in year two.

I sat down and asked myself one simple question. What were the 330 successful entrepreneurs that I had interviewed over the last eleven months doing to generate revenue? I pored over show notes, went to their websites, relistened to countless episodes—and finally the answer smacked me across the head.

The most successful entrepreneurs were offering one amazing solution to one real problem. They had positioned themselves as the "go-to expert" in their area of expertise and were focused on going one inch wide and one mile deep. In other words, they refused to be distracted by anything other than providing the best solution of a real struggle their audience was experiencing.

Their laser focus was inspiring, and I knew the model was the winner.

My next step? I asked my audience, Fire Nation, what their biggest struggle was. As I shared in the previous chapter, I sent out emails, I created a specific podcast episode requesting direct feedback to this very question, I made social media posts and sent private messages, all with the same question, "What is your biggest struggle right now?"

I received a myriad of responses, but a consistent response was a variation of: "We want to create and launch a podcast around our passion and knowledge. Can you help?"

I sat down to ponder what solution I could deliver that would solve this pain point. I asked myself what was missing when I started my podcasting journey a mere fifteen months prior. The answer came to me in a stroke of genius (or what I hoped was): people were intimidated by podcasting because they perceived it would take a ton of time, energy, and bandwidth.

They already felt maxed out with work, family, and everything else they had going on in their world. What if I created a platform that would do all the hard work around podcasting? A platform that allowed my clients to do the bare minimum—record the audio content and send it to me?

The more I thought about this concept, the more fired up I got. This was it! I would create a platform that would do everything minus the actual audio creation. I would call it PodPlatform and it would be awesome! PodPlatform would:

- Host the podcast
- Edit every interview
- Add the intros and outros
- Create the show notes
- Publish the episode on every major directory
- Help the host market the show successfully

I was fired up. In my mind, this service was a no-brainer. I knew these services had a lot of perceived value, and with the right team I could scale this service into profitability. I was already running projected numbers in my mind and they looked great.

This is where I should have gone to my audience and gained proof of concept. I should have presented the idea to my audience and asked for financial commitments up front. If this was something that solved a pain point, Fire Nation would have been happy to pony up a few bucks to lock in this service, which would have provided the proof of concept I never received.

Instead, I put my head down and nose to the grindstone and got to work. I built out a team, locked in a hosting account, trained my team on the various activities they would need to be competent at by launch time, as well as all the other little things it takes to run a service-based business.

Two months went by as I poured more money, time, and effort into PodPlatform. Then came launch day. I was *fired* up.

I composed the email to alert all those whom I pictured chomping at the bit to throw their credit card at me for this amazing service. I scanned the email one time, then pressed *send*.

I eagerly awaited the sales to start rolling in.

Boom!

Immediately a sale came in.

Bam.

Another sale.

Sweet! It was all coming together! It was time to sit back, relax, and watch the money pour in.

I never made another sale during the short life of PodPlatform. It was now forty-eight hours since I had sent the email announcing the opening of PodPlatform. I was in a state of shock.

Two sales? Only two sales? I thought this was what everyone wanted.

Well, I did have two clients and it was time to get to work. Then I saw that one of my clients had just sent me an email.

I opened the message and read the following words: *John, after much consideration I've decided this service isn't for me and I'd like to request a refund.*

Ouch. I'd just lost 50 percent of my clientele.

Spoiler alert . . . my remaining clientele, one person, turned out to be a nightmare. She had a million questions about every step of the process and was never satisfied with my work. The breaking point came when I got an email late one night demanding that I remove the *um* at minute 28:43 of her show that was going live the next morning.

I completed her request and then composed an email saying I was fully refunding her investment and was shutting down the service.

PodPlatform was an utter failure. It was time to pick up the pieces and figure out what I had done wrong. I retraced every step I had taken and was able to identify the exact moment I had veered off the common path to uncommon success.

I had not received proof of concept for my service. My audience wanted to learn how to create and launch a podcast, but PodPlatform was not the solution they needed. I had made a lot of assumptions, sunk a ton of time, energy, bandwidth, and finances into this venture and it had completely bombed.

It was time to go back to the drawing board. Not all the way back, just to the point where I failed to have my audience prove my concept before moving forward.

In hindsight, it was a blessing that only two people ever joined Pod-Platform. Had ten or twenty people joined, PodPlatform would have been just successful enough for me to keep my team busy, serve my clients well, and have a tiny slice of profit at the end of the month. That would have been the real disaster, because it would have consumed months and potentially years of my life, not allowing for any space or time to create something that could become a true success.

Sadly, I see many businesses operating in this manner. They go all in on a model that barely covers the bills yet takes all their time and effort. Their business is considered a success, but I would classify it as a common success.

You and I committed to achieving uncommon success, and the failure of PodPlatform opened the door of possibility and allowed me to retrace my steps, identify what was wrong, make a few adjustments and one small pivot, then launch the solution that resulted in the achievement of financial freedom and fulfillment.

Podcasters' Paradise

A couple of weeks had gone by since I'd closed the doors to PodPlatform. I was running along Mission Bay in San Diego, listening to a podcast and letting my mind drift as to what solution I could craft for my audience. I breathed in the salty breeze and reveled in the warm sun. Being from Maine, the San Diego weather was something I never took for granted.

I glanced up at the swaying palm trees and said to myself, *Wow, this is paradise!* I needed to create an online version of this feeling for podcasters. That's when the name hit me . . . Podcasters' Paradise!

I would create a place where podcasters could go for answers to all their podcasting questions, concerns, and struggles. Podcasters' Paradise would also provide support and guidance from other podcasters (myself included).

This felt right.

However, PodPlatform had felt right too. I wasn't going to make the same mistake twice in a row. I got home and sketched a very simple concept of what I thought Podcasters' Paradise could look like: video tutorials and an online community. Then, I sent an email to my audience with this bare-bones concept of Podcasters' Paradise and a request for their thoughts and suggested additions.

The feedback was immediate and positive. I received some great suggestions. One I implemented immediately was creating a collection of templates for every aspect of podcasting, such as requesting a guest on your show, podcast release forms, locking down a sponsor, and so on.

I was fired up! But as a wizened old veteran of one failed launch, I knew better than to hunker down and create Podcasters' Paradise.

Nope, it was time for some proof of concept. It was time for people to vote with their wallet. I had to separate my cheerleaders from my buyers.

Cheerleaders are those in your audience who wish you the best, hope you succeed, and believe every one of your ideas is a great one. They mean well, but cheerleaders can do serious damage to your business, because cheerleaders are not buyers. When you release a product or service they encouraged you so adamantly to create, they stand on the sidelines and say, "Good luck! I'm sure it will do fantastic. I mean, I'm not gonna to buy it, but I'm sure it will do great!"

I was done creating products and services for cheerleaders. I was committed to creating products and services for *buyers*. People who put their money where their mouth is. People who voted with their wallets, not their kind words. People who invested in themselves and their future.

Having learned my lesson with the failure of PodPlatform, I committed to getting proof of concept for Podcasters' Paradise before spending any time, money, or mental bandwidth. On a Friday, I composed an email thanking everyone for their amazing feedback. I then outlined what Podcasters' Paradise would consist of.

- Video tutorials of how to create, grow, and monetize your podcast
- Sample templates covering every aspect of podcasting
- An online community where people could interact daily, asking myself and the other members questions while receiving guidance and support
- A monthly livestream where I would answer questions, and bring on other top podcasters to share their best tips, tools, and tactics

I finished the email by announcing that the doors to Podcasters' Paradise would open in forty-five days, if I had at least twenty people invest by Sunday at midnight. I incentivized these early birds by sharing that their investment today would be $250 and would include lifetime access to Podcasters' Paradise. Plus, they would be able to provide feedback and direction over the next forty-five days as we built Podcasters' Paradise together.

I also shared that when the doors opened in forty-five days the price point would be $500, so they were locking in a 50 percent discount by investing now. I ended by candidly sharing that if I did not meet the twenty-person quota by Sunday, Podcasters' Paradise would remain nothing more than a dream.

Once again, I held my breath and pressed *send*. Within two hours, I had twenty sales. Proof of concept! By Sunday at midnight, I had thirty-five early bird members in Podcasters' Paradise.

The next forty-five days flew by as I created tutorials and templates on a subject I knew and loved, podcasting. My early birds were a huge help as I asked for their feedback every step of the way and implemented many of their ideas. As promised, Podcasters' Paradise opened to the world on October 31, 2013, and was an immediate success.

I wasn't overly shocked, as I had already achieved proof of concept forty-five days prior. To date, Podcasters' Paradise has welcomed over six thousand members and generated over $5 million in revenue. As big of a failure as PodPlatform was, Podcasters' Paradise was a resounding success.

Every single product and service we've launched since Podcasters' Paradise has followed the same formula of gaining proof of concept before spending time, money, and mental bandwidth creating a solution for our audience.

We've had plenty of ideas fail at the proof of concept phase and even a couple fizzle out soon after launch despite gaining what we believed was proof of concept, because frankly that stuff happens in the entrepreneurial world. The common path to uncommon success is not a straight line to success, but rather a guide to stack the odds in your favor.

You got this!

An Entrepreneur on Fire's Path to Uncommon Success

OMAR ZENHOM AND NICOLE BALDINU ON PROVING THE CONCEPT AND CRAFTING THE SOLUTION

If you define the problem correctly, you almost have the solution. —STEVE JOBS

THE YEAR WAS 2012. Nicole and Omar had been teaching professionally for thirteen years and each had a master's in education. They were over it. Underpaid and overworked, they were ready to set off on their own and create a life of freedom and fulfillment.

In 2013, they launched The $100 MBA with the promise of a practical business training and community for $100. For over eight years they have fulfilled that promise. Every week, Omar and Nicole delivered live training via webinars and offered enrollment in The $100 MBA.

Business was good, with only one issue: each week, Omar was spending hours preparing for one single webinar. He would Frankenstein the entire process, connecting the email marketing to the landing pages to the calendar reminders to the webinar itself. Then he would fire up the webinar, connect to a chat software, run the webinar, upload the recording to Vimeo, secure the access, and send out replays.

The following week, he'd do it all over again.

Being an organized fellow, Omar developed a checklist so he could follow his detailed process every week without having to re-create the wheel. That checklist turned into an *a-ha* moment. Why not package and sell this checklist? Other people were having similar struggles and this was a great solution.

In that moment, *The DIY Webinar Guide* was born. Omar and Nicole were sure they had a winner and poured a ton of time, energy, and effort into making this DIY guide great.

With much fanfare, they launched the guide, celebrated, and waited for the sales to roll in. The sales never rolled in. In total, they made two sales—one to me (which I still look at as a great investment), and one other sale, which promptly turned into a chargeback.

Omar and Nicole were shocked. They were in a similar state as I was in after the failure of PodPlatform. They experienced their Ben Horowitz moment: *Sometimes you must create a bad product to create a great one.*

The DIY Webinar Guide was their bad product moment. Belatedly, they realized people want a done-for-you solution, not a giant Frankenstein checklist.

They scrapped the project and went back to what was working, live webinars and The $100 MBA. Omar had some WordPress development skills and created a plugin to simplify the onerous task of hosting a live webinar each week.

During his webinars, the attendees began to ask what software he was using to run such seamless events. When Omar told them about the plugin, they asked if they could buy access to it: *a-ha* moment number two!

This time, Omar and Nicole would not put a ton of time, energy, and effort into a polished product. They were going to prove the concept first. They put together a bare-bones landing page that listed the features and benefits of the plugin and emailed their tiny email list. They were up front about the fact that the product wouldn't be ready for at least four months, but those who joined now would receive lifetime access.

They capped their first round at 150 people. It sold out in forty-eight hours. They opened another hundred spots and those sold out in twenty-four hours. Finally, Omar and Nicole had achieved proof of concept: WebinarNinja was born.

For four months, Omar and Nicole worked side by side with a single freelance developer, creating the beta version of WebinarNinja. Their early birds proved priceless. Every time Omar and Nicole had a question, their early birds provided answers.

True to their word, WebinarNinja launched four months later. This time, their launch absolutely crushed it. Since 2014, Omar and Nicole have amassed over 15,000 users. Over one million people have attended a WebinarNinja webinar.

Even with all this success, Omar still hosts every sales webinar and demo himself. Their team regularly conducts user interviews and discovery surveys to make sure they are on top of what their best users want. They also have a cancellation form that their team studies every month to see the biggest reasons people are leaving the platform. This ensures they are always working on the top five to ten reasons people leave WebinarNinja.

The three biggest areas they direct their focus toward are:

1. Keeping WebinarNinja a simple, all-in-one platform where you can host a quality webinar fast.
2. High quality support. They will forever remain committed to offering the best support in the industry.
3. Keeping their finger on the pulse of their users so they can ensure WebinarNinja evolves as the needs of the market and their users evolve.

In Omar and Nicole's own words: "Your product solution is only as good as your team, and one of the best things we've done is really understand the customer we are serving and being a part of the community by being a user as well. Be an ambassador to your community."

Thank you, Omar and Nicole.

You can learn more about Omar and Nicole at 100MBA.net and WebinarNinja.com.

Check out your free companion course for added support along *The Common Path to Uncommon Success*: EOFire.com/success-course.

CHAPTER 12

Build Your Funnel

You have to tell a story before you can sell a story.
—BETH COMSTOCK

How many people get married on the first date? How many people buy the first house they see? Of course, these things happen, but they are the exception, not the rule. If you run your business on exceptions, you'll never find uncommon success.

Let's take the example of buying a house. Which real estate agent do you think would be more successful?

One who meets you and says, *"Hi! I'm Mary and I have the perfect house for you. I know we just met and I don't know anything about you and haven't asked you any questions, but just trust me, you're going to love it."*

Or, the agent who says, *"Hi, I'm Maria and here is a pamphlet on the ten biggest mistakes first-time homeowners make. I want to make sure we avoid all those! I'd love to sit down, get to know you, and hear what your dream house would be. Then I'll share my knowledge of the real estate opportunities in this area that would fit your needs. Then we'll take a drive and I will educate you about the different neighborhoods, we'll see some houses, you'll tell me what you like and don't like, and I'll adjust the search accordingly and we'll keep at it till we find your dream home."*

Obviously, Maria crushes it and Mary wonders why she sells zero homes, has zero referrals, and of course makes zero revenue. Sadly, most entrepreneurs treat their avatars like Mary without even realizing it.

When you've identified your big idea, niched down, created your avatar, chosen your platform, locked in your mentor and mastermind, designed your content production plan, created great content, launched, pinpointed your avatar's biggest struggle, and crafted the solution, it is time to build your funnel.

A funnel is the journey your avatar takes from the moment they are introduced to your content for the very first time all the way to becoming a customer, client, or evangelist. The days of "Hi, my name is John, now buy my product" are long gone. In fact, they never existed.

The first thing to know is humans buy from humans. Secondly, humans buy from humans they know, like, and trust.

By following the common path to uncommon success, you know your avatar's biggest struggles. You deliver solutions to these struggles on your platform of choice. You deliver these valuable solutions for free and consistently. As a result, your avatar knows, likes, and trusts you.

Now it's time to build the funnel that will take your avatar on a journey to become your customer. At *Entrepreneurs on Fire*, we have multiple funnels running simultaneously, each delivering specific value based off our avatar's struggles. Each funnel ends with the offer of a product, service, or community.

I'll go into details of a specific funnel of ours that has generated millions of dollars later in this chapter, but first let me show you how our struggling real estate agent (Mary) could turn her business around by following the common path to uncommon success.

Another month has gone by, and once again, Mary has made zero sales. Complaining about her "bad luck" to her friend over lunch one day, Mary claims she is going to quit the industry.

Her friend recommends a book called *The Common Path to Uncommon Success.* "Sarah swears by this book, and she has been crushing it in business recently!" Mary's friend shares. Having nothing to lose, Mary buys the book and commits to going all in.

After reading the first chapter, Mary realizes she has much to learn. She confirms her big idea is real estate, but realizes she's never considered niching down. Mary goes for a walk and tries to identify a void that needs to be filled in her real estate market. Her mind drifts to her younger years.

Her father was in the Army and they moved around a *lot.* Every time they moved to a new area, they would meet with a real estate agent, buy a home, and a couple years later use the same agent when it came time to sell and move to the next Army base. Her parents had done quite well with their real estate transactions and were now comfortably retired and living off their savings and passive real estate income.

Mary immediately thought of the nearby military base. It was massive and there were always military families coming and going. After a quick search online, Mary could not find a single real estate agent who was focused on serving these military men and women. *Boom!* Mary found a void that needed to be filled.

Next, Mary crafted her avatar, who was a thirty-five-year-old woman whose husband was a military officer. They had three kids and a dog and were looking for a four-bedroom house with a large backyard.

Mary found a mentor who was where she wanted to be in the real estate world, dug into her savings, and invested in her three-month program.

Mary started a real estate mastermind with two of her peers and they began to meet weekly.

Mary was on a roll. She decided to start a podcast focused on real estate tips for military families and began releasing two episodes per week, sharing solutions to the major problems faced by military families during a move.

Mary also went to the local military base and connected with the housing affairs department. She asked what value she could provide, and after a short discussion it became obvious that one of the biggest questions asked by incoming military families was information on the best neighborhoods to live in and why.

Mary created a pamphlet that answered these questions and printed out hundreds. She delivered these pamphlets to the housing affairs department, who began to include them in the folders they mailed to military families who were being assigned to their base. After a couple weeks, Mary's phone began ringing.

When she picked up, it was her avatar on the other line sharing how she had received Mary's pamphlet, was very grateful, and wanted to set up showings for when they arrived the following week.

Before, every client was a battle. Every client had so many options and Mary was offering nothing special or unique. Now it was different. Mary's avatars were presold. They looked at Mary as the go-to expert for military relocation and were so thankful for the free value she had provided via her pamphlet and podcast.

Reciprocity is real. When you provide massive value for free, people look for a way to reciprocate. In Mary's case, her clients reciprocated with unquestioned loyalty and referrals. Before she knew it, Mary was forced to hire a secretary to take calls and book appointments, as well as a showing agent to take the overflow of clients she was experiencing.

Mary was finally on the common path to uncommon success.

Where did it start? With her identifying a niche that was not being served properly and serving it ten times better than her competition even dreamed of.

Mary had built her funnel, and now her only focus was to keep feeding it. The common path to uncommon success was finally a reality for Mary, and she was *on fire*!

My Funnel

It was January of 2014. Podcasters' Paradise had been open for two months and had generated over $100,000 in sales. The sales were great, but I could see the writing on the wall. The initial launch was successful and everyone in my audience who had been waiting for a course like this had joined.

Now the real work began. Sales were slowing and I had to figure out a way to keep a steady flow of qualified leads coming my way. I needed to build a funnel.

I needed to find people who were interested in podcasting, provide them free value, and take them on a journey that ended with an offer to join Podcasters' Paradise. That journey would consist of delivering massive free value every step along the funnel, until presenting them with the opportunity to join Podcasters' Paradise.

I sat down to build the perfect podcast funnel. My first step was to identify where my current leads came from. The answer was simple: *Entrepreneurs on Fire.*

I knew a certain percentage of my listeners wanted to learn more about podcasting but were not ready to invest in a premium course and community. I had to create a step in between to provide them value on podcasting and get them fired up to learn more.

I decided to create a free podcast course. This course would be high quality. It would consist of video tutorials and templates that would teach how to create and launch your podcast.

I got to work. Using screen flow, keynote, and my webcam, I created five video tutorials that were a combination of me on camera and presentation slides. This allowed me to connect with the viewers directly through video while delivering value via keynote.

When creating a free course, it's important to deliver a clear result. Creating a free course of fluff will only annoy people and send them elsewhere for the content they desire.

With my free podcast course, I was providing high-quality training with a clear result. By the end of this course, you will have created and launched your podcast.

Once the free course was complete, I began to promote it on all my platforms. At the end of every *Entrepreneurs on Fire* episode, I created this call to action: *Hey, Fire Nation, I hope you enjoyed today's episode with*

Tim. By the way, if you are listening to this episode and thinking you might like to start your very own podcast, I have great news for you. I've created a completely free course that will teach you how to create and launch your podcast! Simply visit FreePodcastCourse.com to get started today. See you there!

When people visited FreePodcastCourse.com, they entered their email to unlock the free course. Soon, hundreds were signing up every week. People would complete the course at their own pace, and before I knew it, I was getting dozens of emails from people who had successfully launched their podcast by following the tutorials of the Free Podcast Course.

This is when this funnel began to bear fruit. I delivered on my promise. Free Podcast Course taught how to create and launch your podcast. Now that my students had successfully launched, they were looking for the next solution to their new struggle.

That struggle? Growing their podcast audience and monetizing. I presented the solution.

> Join Podcasters' Paradise and I will teach you how to grow your podcast audience. Once you have a large audience, Podcasters' Paradise will provide the training for you to monetize!

Soon, people who completed Free Podcast Course were joining Podcasters' Paradise that very same day!

Did 100 percent of those who completed Free Podcast Course join Podcasters' Paradise? No. Not everyone will be in the position to accept your offer when presented, but by building a funnel and delivering on a valuable promise, you are creating a very powerful emotion: reciprocity.

It could be weeks, months, or even years for the time to be right for someone to take the next step and join your course, community, or program. The free value you're providing within your funnel are seeds that will bloom at various times in the upcoming years.

As time went on, I continued to add layers and value to the funnel. I created a twenty-episode podcast called *Free Podcast Course Podcast.* I created a sixty-minute webinar training called The Podcast Masterclass. I crafted a series of fifteen emails packed with podcasting tips, tools, and tactics. All roads led to one destination, Podcasters' Paradise.

Over the years, I've received messages from people who attended seven Podcast Masterclasses before joining, or read each email three times, or took Free Podcast Course five times.

When you provide free, valuable, and consistent content and build a funnel that presents an irresistible offer, it's only a matter of time before you'll see the fruits of your labor.

An Entrepreneur on Fire's Path to Uncommon Success

RUSSELL BRUNSON ON BUILDING A SALES FUNNEL

*Whoever can spend the most money
to acquire a customer wins.*
—DAN KENNEDY

RUSSELL WAS ON TOP of the world. He was selling a $27 DVD on how to make potato guns, and his advertising costs were less than $10 per sale. Russell was making over $17 per transaction and thought his path to riches was bright. It wasn't.

Google raised its ad rates and suddenly it was costing Russell $50 to make a single sale, which meant he was losing money every time someone bought his product. Russell had to figure something out quick. That something turned out to be funnels, and it changed Russell's life forever.

Before we dive deeper into Russell's story, let's take a step back. *What exactly is a sales funnel?* Simply put, a sales funnel is a customer's journey from the moment they are introduced to your initial solution all the way through to your final solution.

Sales funnels have been around for a long time. The most successful companies in history have leveraged sales funnels to fuel their profits.

Think about buying a car. Lead generation begins with commercials, billboards, and events. These advertisements get you in the door where a salesperson will help you choose a car. Most people think that's where the funnel ends, but it's just the beginning. When the salesperson takes you to their office to sign the contract, the real funnel begins.

This is where the salespeople make most of their commissions and the dealership makes most of their profits. *Do you want a warranty? Mud flaps? Undercarriage protection from all that salt on the roads? How about an upgrade to better tires?* These are some of the up-sells car dealerships use to bring in the real dough.

McDonald's uses the same strategy. They advertise the mouthwatering Big Mac. Isn't that exactly what you want for lunch? *Yum!* Then, when you order the Big Mac, you hear the words *"Would you like fries and a Coke with that?"* This is McDonald's up-sell and allows them to break even (or even lose money) advertising the Big Mac. They make their money on the fries and Coke!

Now let's talk about Amazon. In the early days of the internet, people weren't thinking about sales funnels. They had a static sales page with one product for sale. Then along came Amazon and the retail sales funnel was perfected. When you visit Amazon and buy a book, you are immediately shown *"people who bought this book also bought these items."* Amazon is strategically analyzing their data and promoting the most likely items this shopper would buy next. Amazon is winning because they know the buyer's next logical problem and control every step of the process.

Back to Russell and his struggling potato gun business. If he was going to avoid bankruptcy, Russell would have to figure out how to become profitable again. Luckily, Russell had a friend reach out who was selling similar products online and who had discovered the "secret" to increasing profit margins.

He shared the concept of "the up-sell." The up-sell increased the average cart value by offering your buyers the next logical solution after buying your product. Russell's friend was converting one out of every three customers into an up-sell, allowing him to remain profitable even with rising advertising costs.

Russell thought about the next logical step his buyers took after buying his DVD. They went to Home Depot to buy the supplies to make the actual potato gun. Russell did some research and found a company nearby that sold potato gun kits. They formed a partnership where every person who bought Russell's DVD was then offered a potato gun kit. Russell would earn a $200 commission for each kit sold.

One out of every three customers began buying the kit, which brought Russell's average cart value up to $93.66. Russell could now afford the $50 per sale advertising cost and still profit $43.66 per sale.

This was the moment Russell fell in love with the concept of funnels and the customer journey. Russell started applying these principles in other markets with the same results. They would study the customer journey and discover the next logical step after every purchase. This strategy allowed Russell to outspend all his competitors in advertising because his average cart value was always the highest in the industry when all the up-sells were factored in.

When creating a funnel, you need to ask, "What is the next obvious problem that needs to be solved?"

Let's use the example of six-pack abs. When someone lands on your sales page looking for six-pack abs, your job is to convince them that your product can provide the solution to their problem. If you're successful and the person buys your product, they have not yet achieved a six-pack, but in their mind they have, as the only thing between them and six-pack abs is a little bit of time and your product.

If your up-sell is to buy a book on six-pack abs, it will fail because they already have the tool they need to get the six-pack abs, and why would they need to buy a duplicate product? Instead, you have to ask, "What is the next logical solution they need?" It might be, "What are the supplements needed to get that six-pack faster?" or "What are the foods I need to avoid to speed up this process?" Remember, when you sell a product and solve a problem, a new problem appears.

Your funnel is built around the question "How do I solve that next problem?" In Russell's own words: "Strategically thinking through your customer journey, that is, your sales funnel, will help you make more money from every person that enters your world. This will allow you to spend more money to acquire a customer, and as my mentor Dan Kennedy says, 'Whoever can spend the most money to acquire a customer wins.'"

Thank you, Russell Brunson.

You can learn more about Russell at ClickFunnels.com.

Check out your free companion course for added support along *The Common Path to Uncommon Success*: EOFire.com/success-course.

CHAPTER 13

Diversify Your
Revenue Streams

*You don't have to see the whole staircase,
just take the first step.*
—MARTIN LUTHER KING JR.

W e've all heard the wise words *don't put all your eggs in one basket.*
Those words ring true today. We live in an incredibly dynamic
world. Opportunities are changing and evolving at a rapid rate.

What's hot today can be ice cold tomorrow. What could be crushing it for you this month could produce a goose egg the following month. The common path to uncommon success is not about finding one thing and crushing it, but in building a diversified business that has a foundation that will see you through the economic cycles and shifts to come.

Uncommon success means that you will thrive in the good times and survive during the lean. Uncommon success means you must create diversified streams of revenue so you can adapt when the economy, Mother Nature, or life in general throws a curveball.

The common path to uncommon success will guide you in identifying your big idea, discovering the niche, and creating the best solution to your avatar's struggle. That will allow you to gain traction and momentum.

As your audience grows, you need to engage one-on-one at every opportunity. In chapter 10, we went over the four questions to ask your audience to pinpoint their biggest struggle. That exercise concluded with you choosing the solution to provide. You created the solution and built the funnel and now it's time to identify your next step.

It's time to get back on calls with your audience and ask these five questions. The five questions are like those in chapter 10, but the goal of these conversations is to keep your finger on the pulse of your audience and reveal potential ideas that will allow you to diversify your income streams.

1. How did you discover my content?
2. What do you want to see more of?
3. What do you want to see less of?
4. What is your biggest struggle right now?
5. If I could give you a magic button that when pressed would reveal the perfect solution to that problem, what would that solution look like?

Now let's go over each question, why it's important, and how these conversations will help you reveal other income streams.

1. **How did you discover my content?** When you are creating free, valuable, and consistent content, you will be adding new members to your audience on a consistent basis. It is critical to know the top ways people are discovering your content in order to focus your marketing efforts in those areas.
2. **What do you want to see more of?** As your business matures, there will be slight adjustments to your content

and the way you deliver it that may not be perceptible to you as the content creator. This question will ensure that you remain aware of why your listeners are drawn to your content and what they want to see more of.

3. **What do you want to see less of?** Content that your listeners loved when you started may not be as appealing as it once was. This question will ensure that you spot negative trends early so you can adjust and pivot as necessary.

4. **What is your biggest struggle right now?** This question will always be the most important question you can ask your audience. It allows you to keep your finger on the pulse of what really matters to the people consuming your content and continuously provide the most pressing and important solutions. Your audience's struggles will evolve as your business evolves. Additionally, once you've perfected the initial solution, it's time to add to a suite of solutions, thus diversifying your revenue streams and protecting yourself from future vulnerabilities.

5. **If I could give you a magic button that when pressed would reveal the perfect solution to that problem, what would that solution look like?** This is a special question because it gives your audience the opportunity to share their thoughts and ideas of what a perfect solution would look like. This is like when Henry Ford would walk his assembly lines and ask his workers what they would do to improve the operation. Sometimes, unless you are living the struggle, you can't identify what the best solution would look like. Give your audience a chance to reveal pearls of wisdom that would have otherwise remained unknown.

In summation, it is important to remember that this world is a crazy, ever-evolving, fragile place.

All the opportunity in the future lies in the unpredictable world we live in, so embrace it.

I've heard many people share some version of the below:

John, I can't believe I missed the podcast/snapchat/Instagram/
TikTok [fill in the blank of the next great thing].

My response is always the same . . .

Keep your eyes on the horizon, because the "next big thing" is always
coming and there will be an opportunity for you to go all in and
create something special.

I wasn't the first person to create a podcast. I launched my podcast eight years after the first episode was published. But I was the first person to go all in on the platform and create a daily podcast interviewing the world's most inspiring entrepreneurs.

Dominating that niche elevated me to the top of the podcast pyramid and cemented my status as an authority and expert on the platform. When you achieve that status, the snowball effect takes on a life of its own and your authority grows both with and without your efforts.

For example, once I had achieved a certain level of success in the podcasting space, outlets like *Forbes, Inc., Fast Company,* and other media giants began writing about my success and linking to my website, products, and services. This exemplifies the power of the first-mover advantage.

On the common path, you'll attain the first-mover advantage and ride that wave all the way to uncommon success.

Diversifying My Revenue Streams

Over the years, we've created multiple seven-figure funnels. A common question I'm asked is, "John, how did you come up with all those great ideas?" The truth? I didn't. I simply followed the common path to uncommon success.

I built an audience who trusted me because I provided them free, valuable, and consistent content. I asked what their biggest struggle was. I proved the concept and crafted the solution. Then, using the tactics discussed in the previous chapter, I built a funnel that took my audience on a journey where the only reasonable conclusion was the product, service, or community I offered them.

Podcasters' Paradise quickly grew into a seven-figure funnel and that funnel was clicking on all cylinders. It was time to look for that next step.

I analyzed our business. What was working? Where was our revenue coming from? What was making the biggest impact?

The answer was clear: webinars. Our live webinars were converting so well that we began to host them on a weekly basis. We created systems and processes to ensure they were well attended and ran smoothly. We began to receive a lot of questions around webinars . . .

- What platform did we use to host our webinars?
- What did our pre- and post-email sequences look like?
- How did we get so many people to attend so regularly?

These were the questions that gave us our next *a-ha* moment. We had created a great system to deliver regular webinars to our podcasting audience—why not teach others that system? This could be the first step to diversifying our income while providing even more value to our audience.

After a little brainstorming, we decided to call the potential course "Webinar on Fire: Create a Webinar That Converts." Following the common path to uncommon success, we offered a presale of Webinar on Fire to prove the concept before investing time, money, and bandwidth into such a venture. Fortunately, the demand was there and the presales rolled in, proving to us that there was a ready and willing market of individuals looking to create amazing webinars for their audience.

Webinar on Fire proved to be an incredible and complementary revenue stream to Podcasters' Paradise. Over the years, Webinar on

Fire has generated hundreds of thousands of dollars and helped our business grow financially stronger and more secure.

When you follow the common path to uncommon success, you are building a strong foundation—a foundation that will support diversified revenue streams so you can adjust and adapt as needed.

You don't have to know all the building blocks in your foundation now. They'll be revealed as you continue along the common path to uncommon success.

This is the common path to uncommon success, not the confusing path to rocky results. Trust the process, trust yourself, and, above all, take that first step!

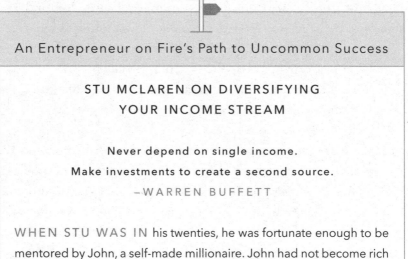

An Entrepreneur on Fire's Path to Uncommon Success

STU MCLAREN ON DIVERSIFYING
YOUR INCOME STREAM

Never depend on single income.
Make investments to create a second source.
—WARREN BUFFETT

WHEN STU WAS IN his twenties, he was fortunate enough to be mentored by John, a self-made millionaire. John had not become rich overnight, but over time. He taught Stu the difference between short-term riches and long-term wealth. Short-term riches are here today, gone tomorrow. Long-term wealth lasts a lifetime.

John ran a very successful seminar business that produced short-term riches. This provided cash flow. John leveraged this cash flow to fuel long-term wealth in the form of real estate.

For the first half of his career, John was a car mechanic with zero cash flow. It wasn't until his forties that he entered the seminar business and real estate investing. John invested in residential properties, commercial offices, and other income-producing real estate ventures. Over time, his real estate portfolio grew and the revenue it produced began to snowball.

His seminar business taught others how he was building wealth in real estate and how they could too. John took the time to pass his knowledge down to Stu, who now thinks about diversification in two ways, online and offline.

Online is how Stu generates the short-term riches that he can invest in offline wealth creation. Stu's short-term riches come in the form of selling information online, such as books, courses, memberships, software, coaching, masterminds, and live events. These short-term riches come in the form of onetime sales and recurring sales.

Of the two, Stu focuses on recurring. Examples of recurring revenue streams are when people pay a monthly fee to retain access to coaching, masterminds, or software. In Stu's experience, the more recurring revenue streams you have, the more stable your business is.

When it comes to diversification of his business, Stu goes deep in one specific segment of the market and *stacks the momentum*. Stacking the momentum allows you to serve the same market with similar offers so you are not always re-creating the wheel. This comes back to becoming the acknowledged leader in your space and providing multiple solutions for your audience in your area of expertise.

Offline, Stu focuses on two types of real estate. Stu likes long-term residential rentals because they provide steady and dependable income. Stu likes short-term luxury rentals because they have a premium price point and higher profit margins.

The beauty of diversification is that if an income stream dries up, you are still able to rely on your other revenue streams to keep your business afloat while you wait out the storm or course correct. In Stu's own words: "The key is to stack the momentum by staying in the same market and going deep to discover more ways to serve your audience at a higher level. This allows you to have a diversification in your offerings with a slant toward recurring revenue streams like memberships, masterminds, and software. Then, use your short-term riches to invest offline in long-term rentals and short-term luxury rentals to build life-time wealth."

Thank you, Stu McLaren.

You can learn more about Stu at Stu.me.

Check out your free companion course for added support along *The Common Path to Uncommon Success*: EOFire.com/success-course.

CHAPTER 14

Increase Your Traffic

You are out of business if you don't have a prospect.
—ZIG ZIGLAR

I f you've been following the common path to uncommon success, you're on *fire*! You've built a fantastic foundation and are impacting the world. Now, you need to put your foot on the gas and increase the traffic you're generating. There will always be paid opportunities to increase your traffic, whether through advertising on Facebook, Google, or any of the latest and greatest lead generators in the online space.

On the common path to uncommon success, we'll keep our focus on evergreen strategies that will always work. You have your platform; now it's time to use it.

Let's use YouTube as an example. People who watch YouTube videos are already the converted. They know the platform. They've voluntarily raised their hands as people who enjoy consuming video content. So, all you need to do is create great video content, sit back, and let your avatars beat a path to your doorstep, right?

In the movie *Field of Dreams*, Kevin Costner is famous for saying, "If you build it, they will come." Sadly, the real world is not the *Field of*

Dreams. A more accurate quote would be, "If you build it, most people won't care."

Harsh words, but true. I think a more accurate quote is, "If you build it, they won't care until you *make* them aware." How do you make them aware? Not by creating content in your bubble and staying inside your bubble. You need to create great content and then *collaborate* with other creators in your niche who are creating great content for your avatars.

In this example, you need to find other YouTubers whose audience is full of your avatars, reach out to them, and collaborate. You need to find a way to add value to their world and allow them to add value to yours. Maybe you could create an amazing piece of content for their channel, and they can do the same. Maybe you could interview them on your channel, and be interviewed for theirs.

This is creating a win-win relationship and will allow their audience to become aware of you and vice versa. Before you overthink this, please remember the following: *All ships rise in a high tide.*

You must approach this task with a mindset of abundance. There will be people who have no desire to collaborate; simply move on to the next opportunity. They are displaying a mindset of scarcity and there is no need to sink to their level.

Abundance is the world you want to live in, and there are plenty of creators who feel the same. Open your arms, open your heart, and find others who are at a similar place in their journey to collaborate and commingle audiences with.

How I Increased My Traffic

Convert the converted. These are words I live by. When I launched *Entrepreneurs on Fire* in 2012, podcasting was *not* on fire like it is today. I could have spent considerable time, energy, and effort trying to change people's habits, introduce them to something different, and beg them to insert podcasts into their daily routines, but that would have been a mighty struggle.

Podcast listeners listen to podcasts.
–JOHN LEE DUMAS

Instead, I chose to convert the converted. People who listened to podcasts *loved* listening to podcasts. They were converts. They had their favorite podcast app on their phone, they had specific times of the day dedicated to listening, whether that be while they commuted to work, hit the gym, or any number of other activities.

I focused my marketing efforts on those individuals. I knew the average podcast listener subscribed to seven shows, so I set out to become one of the seven for those who listened to podcasts about business and entrepreneurship.

Below is the step-by-step process I used to increase the traffic to *Entrepreneurs on Fire* ten times over the course of two years. It was a lot of effort, but it was the *right* kind of effort and I had a lot of fun along the way.

JLD's step-by-step process for igniting podcast traffic:

1. I went to Apple Podcast directory and viewed the top two hundred podcasts in the business section.
2. I documented every interview-based podcast.
3. I studied their last ten episodes and listened to one entire episode.
4. If I felt I could add value to their show, I clicked on the *website* link right below their logo.
5. On their website, I clicked on the *about* button to learn more about the podcast host and their business.
6. Then I clicked on the *contact* button.
7. Then I filled out their contact form.

Hi XXX, my name is John Lee Dumas and I am the host of the podcast *Entrepreneurs on Fire*. I've been checking out your podcast and I must say I am quite impressed. I just got done listening to your recent episode titled XXX and my favorite takeaway was XXX. I noticed over the last ten episodes you've talked about a lot of great topics, but you haven't focused on this topic, XXX, which happens to be my area of expertise. I would love to provide value on this to your audience, and to make this an even easier yes, here is a proposed title for the episode with some bullet points for the interview flow. As I mentioned earlier, I am a podcast host and would also love to have you on my show to share your knowledge and expertise with my audience, Fire Nation. In fact, we could schedule an hour block over the next week or two and take thirty minutes each to interview each other, a two for one! Plus, as a podcast host, I know how important it is for your guests to share your episodes when they go live so you can count on me sharing this episode with my entire audience! Here is my scheduler link if you'd like to find a time that works for you, or please reply with your scheduler and I'll happily find a time for us!

—John Lee Dumas of *Entrepreneurs on Fire*

PS: I also know how important ratings and reviews are for podcasts so I gave you a well-deserved 5-star rating and review. Keep creating amazing content and I hope we connect soon!

That pitch will net you *hundreds* of interviews on other podcasts, as well as plenty for yours as well! I currently receive over four hundred pitches a month of people wanting to be a guest on *Entrepreneurs on Fire*. The above pitch would instantly become one of the top five pitches I have *ever* received. Ever.

This is why it's important to do things that don't scale. The more personal and specific you are with your outreach, the more success you'll have. Would you rather send out four hundred boilerplate pitches with a .01 percent success rate or twenty personal ones with a 60 percent success rate?

I thought so.

This exact process ensured I was a guest on at least ten other podcasts every month. Every time I was a guest, I delivered the best value I possibly could, built a great relationship with the other podcast host, and my call to action at the end of every interview was a request to check out my show, *Entrepreneurs on Fire.*

This exposure is the single most effective way I got out the word about *Entrepreneurs on Fire.* I built it, I went out and recruited the converted, *then* they came.

There are a lot of ways to grow your traffic, and my recommendation is to test them all, track the results, and focus on those that work best. The above strategy needs to be a part of your strategic growth plan if you create content. Think about your avatar, where they currently are, how you can best access them, and how you can add value to their world so they will seek out your content and become part of your tribe.

An Entrepreneur on Fire's Path to Uncommon Success

BILLY GENE ON INCREASING YOUR TRAFFIC

A man who stops advertising to save money
is like a man who stops a clock to save time.
—HENRY FORD

BILLY GENE is not afraid to offend people. So much so that his podcast is the aptly named *Billy Gene Offends the Internet.* Billy's entire strategy to increase traffic can be summed up in two words. *Spend money.*

Yes, it's counterintuitive, but Billy assures you it's the fastest way to accomplish your goal. Right now, you might be thinking to yourself, *"Easy for you to say, Mr. Rich Pants Billy."* Rich Pants Billy gets it.

He knows what it feels like not to have money. When he started out, Billy was more than $50,000 in debt. He had a bank shut down his account and block him, twice. For a long time, Billy's life consisted of overdraft fees, late charges, and a negative account balance.

Billy likes to joke, "If you haven't seen negative $400 in your bank account, you ain't livin'." He knows what it feels like to read a book like this where the advice is *spend money to increase your traffic* when you have none. It feels like a slap in the face and a waste of time.

Here's how it's not. Billy offers you $5 to stand outside of his business and spin a sign for the next four hours. You need the $5, so you do it. Because of your sign-spinning, Billy gets six people to come into his store who buy stuff and he makes an extra $100 on the day. All for a $5 advertising spend.

Did Billy make money, or did he lose money? Billy made money. Billy's key to advertising: *Make your money back as soon as possible, preferably the same day.*

When Billy evaluates an advertising opportunity, he identifies how he can make his money back almost immediately. This is why Billy loves online advertising. With the right ad, you can reach up to one thousand people online for $5.

The question is, can you sell one of those one thousand people a product or service that will generate $20, $30, or even $50? More importantly, can you make that sale on the same day? The whole game with increasing your traffic is buying it and making it back the same day.

Fast-forward to today—Billy may spend upward of $50,000 in a single day. How can he do that? Billy always asks for the sale. Most people are afraid to ask for the sale. They're afraid to ask people to buy something. They want to create free content and build goodwill with their audience and bide their time.

Why? Because it's safe. Because it feels better. Because it's in their comfort zone.

Billy's secret to reaching more people is to ask them to buy every single time. Then he makes more sales and has more money to buy more traffic.

How do record labels make money? They pay to have their artists put on billboards, on the radio, and on the cover of *Vogue*. The label knows they'll make back way more than their advertising costs when the artist goes big.

Companies buy Super Bowl commercials because they know their sales are going to increase.

Fortune 500 companies spend billions in advertising because they have decades of data showing them it's the best way to increase their profits.

Here's how you can turn $10 into a $300 monthly advertising budget. If you spend $10 a day on bringing traffic to your offer and make $20, you can use the same $10 the following day and do it all over again. Thirty days later, you've used the same $10 for a $300 advertising budget. All from the same $10 bill.

When you make your money back fast, you can spend it again.

What if your limiting belief is "I have nothing to sell"? Then sell someone else's product or service for a commission. In Billy's own words: "You're never stuck, you're just not being creative enough and a lack of creativity will put you out of business, and so will boring."

Thank you, Billy Gene.

You can learn more about Billy Gene at BillyGeneIsMarketing.com.

Check out your free companion course for added support along *The Common Path to Uncommon Success*: EOFire.com/success-course.

CHAPTER 15

Implement Systems and Build a Team

*Every system is perfectly designed
to get the results it gets.*
—DONALD BERWICK

Those of us on the common path to uncommon success are committed to putting in the reps. We do the work. We get stuff done. As our business matures, we implement systems and build teams that allow us to grow and scale.

But like everything else, there is a time and a place for everything. I waited until now to talk about systems team building for a reason. It's critical to know your business from the inside out before you start to implement systems and build the team that will allow you to grow and scale.

We need to understand how every facet of our business operates. Henry Ford knew how to build a car from scratch. He had done so many times. Only after he fully mastered every step of the process did he implement an assembly line to make cars faster, better, and more efficiently.

Picture Henry Ford, walking up and down the assembly line, studying every step in the process, making tweaks here, adjustments there, and taking pride in every car that rolled off the line. You are the Henry Ford of your business. You need to understand how the sauce is made to ensure a high-quality product is always served to your audience.

The good news? You're on the common path to uncommon success. You've put in the work. You've rolled up your sleeves and you understand every part of the process.

Now it's time to grow. It's time to scale. It's time to implement systems and build your team.

But how? One step at time . . .

Your first step in creating the systems and building the team that will allow you to grow and scale is to write down everything you do over the course of a week. Be diligent. Keep track of every task you perform and by the end of the week you should have a comprehensive list.

Your next step is to separate the tasks into two lists. List one will contain all the tasks you'll repeat the following week and list two consists of the onetime tasks you will not repeat.

Dispose of list two.

Now rearrange list one from most time-consuming to least time-consuming.

Start at the top and identify one of your most time-consuming tasks you'd like to create a system for. Next, write out the step-by-step process of how you accomplish that task. Then, look at the step-by-step process and see if you can identify any unnecessary steps. Remove every unnecessary step until you have the most lean and efficient process you can create.

Next, create a video of you talking and walking through this process. You can use a free service like Loom for this. Once you've finished, label the video correctly and store it in a folder on your computer labeled *Systems*.

Every week, your goal should be to create at least one training following the steps above. In a short time, you'll have a library of tutorials of your most time-consuming tasks. When you begin to build your team, you'll have the training ready for them to consume early and often. Also, if you ever need to replace a team member in the future or onboard someone new, your library of trainings awaits.

This process will allow you to create systems for your business in a very effective manner, as you'll be focusing on the most repetitive and time-consuming tasks first, and working your way down the list.

Now let's move onto building your team.

Implementing Our Systems and Assembling "Team Fire"

It was February of 2013. *Entrepreneurs on Fire* had just turned six months old and we were growing fast. We had just crossed 100,000 listens a month. I had recently returned from my first speaking engagement at New Media Expo in Las Vegas. I had reached a tipping point where more people were reaching out to be a guest on *Entrepreneurs on Fire* than I had spots available.

> I alone cannot change the world, but I can cast
> a stone across the water to create many ripples.
> —MOTHER TERESA

The founder of a podcast sponsorship company had reached out and was going to work on getting sponsors for my show! Visitors to my website were on the rise, email subscriptions were increasing daily, my social media following was steadily climbing. Everything seemed to be clicking.

The time felt right and I knew I was ready. I was ready to build Team Fire.

When you are operating as a solopreneur, you can only do so much. I had spent the previous nine months (three months pre-launch and six months post) learning every aspect of growing a podcast and on-line brand. I knew what actions had to be taken every day and I knew how I wanted them done.

I was getting to the point where my plate was overflowing. If I tried to add more to my plate, the core essentials of *Entrepreneurs on Fire* would suffer. I knew my priority was to be the host of *Entrepreneurs on Fire*. My primary job was interviewing successful and inspiring entre-preneurs. Nobody could take over my primary job, but all my other daily tasks could be outsourced.

I read Chris Ducker's book *Virtual Freedom* and took pages of notes. *Virtual Freedom* laid out the exact process I needed to follow to make my first hire and build out my team.

I knew the first role I needed to fill: a social media manager. I knew social media was going to be a big part of growing my brand and in-creasing awareness of *EOF*, but I couldn't grow my social media pres-ence properly and be the best host of *Entrepreneurs on Fire* I could be.

I used Virtual Staff Finder to begin my search and submitted the type of experience and skill set I was looking for. Within three days, I was provided with three applicants who fit the exact description I was looking for. I interviewed them separately on Zoom and gave each a task to see their skill set in action. After receiving the com-pleted tasks, there was a clear winner. I made my first hire for Team Fire and it felt great!

Now that I had a full-time virtual assistant, it was time to start off-loading my social media tasks. I created video tutorials of the daily tasks I wanted done, answered my VA's questions as they came up, and provided feedback on the work she was producing. Within a week, my VA was running all my social media channels with zero supervision and I could focus on other parts of my business that needed attention.

A couple of months later, I convinced my girlfriend, Kate, to join the team and take over several operations in the business. Over the next few years, we added two more VAs to streamline our operation and scale to new heights. We are a lean team, but we all know our roles and execute them with pride.

Creating systems and building a team does not happen overnight, but if you work at it steadily and consistently, you'll be incredibly proud of the business you've created on your path to uncommon success.

You got this!

An Entrepreneur on Fire's Path to Uncommon Success

AMY PORTERFIELD ON IMPLEMENTING SYSTEMS AND BUILDING A TEAM

Alone we can do so little; together we can do so much.
—HELEN KELLER

AMY PORTERFIELD calls her virtual team small but mighty and wouldn't have it any other way. In 2009, Amy left corporate to launch her own online business. She vowed to never build a large team. She was done with the corporate environment and all their rules, policies, and guidelines.

For years, Amy kept that vow. She launched multiple courses and communities, and before she knew it, Amy was serving thousands of students. Amy knew if she was going to keep growing revenue and support her students at the highest level, she would have to build a team.

Step by step, Amy assembled her dream team. There have been plenty of mistakes along the way, but Amy hopes you can learn from her successes as well as her failures while building your team.

Today, Amy has eighteen full-time employees and five independent contractors. To run her team effectively, Amy set up four departments:

a marketing department, a content development department, a community department, and an operations department.

Amy hired a director to run each department. Every week, Amy meets with her four directors to discuss business operations. The four directors are the only people Amy directly manages. The directors have managers and coordinators below them, and this tiered structure ensures no one is managing too many people at once.

Each quarter, Amy will meet with her directors in person for two days.

During this forty-eight-hour blitz, they discuss the goals for the quarter, what went wrong last quarter, what needs to be fixed, how they can improve the business, and the performance of each employee.

Upon their return, the updated quarterly and annual goals are announced to make sure her team is always on the same page and moving in the right direction.

To communicate, the team uses Slack. This is where announcements are made and fun conversations can happen.

For all things business, Asana is the only tool used. Asana is where the action items are listed, projects are tracked, and tasks are controlled. Amy's phrase for this is: *Business happens in Asana*.

When it comes to hiring, Amy and her team have worked very hard to dial in a process that works. They recruit talent that might not have otherwise applied to keep their team diverse and inclusive. Additionally, Amy works with an HR and DEI (diversity, equity, and inclusion) consultant. During the interview process, Amy and her directors determine if the person would be a good culture add.

Not a culture fit, a culture *add*. A culture fit would mean they are only hiring people that are like those already on the team. They want to hire people who can add experience and insights that only a diverse team can create.

The next step is a test run. The test run is designed to see how the interviewee works and if they can work on a deadline.

The last step is the in-person interview with each level of management.

Once hired, there is a ninety-day "at will employment." This means that both the employee and the employer can terminate the relationship at will. During these ninety days, Amy has a detailed onboarding process. It includes a complete plan of what is expected every week. This ensures the employee can be eased into the business instead of feeling like they are drinking from a firehose.

Once the ninety-day test is passed, the employee receives health insurance, flexible time off, a "fun only" team retreat each year, and a 20 percent bonus at the end of the year if the business's profit goals are met. There are no annual evaluations. You are evaluated as needed. This ensures everyone knows exactly where they stand and fosters a family environment.

In Amy's own words: "Email is the death of the entrepreneur. Communications happen in Slack, business happens in Asana. No exceptions."

Thank you, Amy Porterfield.

You can learn more about Amy at AmyPorterfield.com.

Check out your free companion course for added support along *The Common Path to Uncommon Success*: EOFire.com/success-course.

CHAPTER 16

Create Affiliate Partnerships

To have an impact on your audience,
you must understand their pain points.
—NEIL PATEL

W e've talked about how understanding your avatar's pain points is a key ingredient in the common path to uncommon success. Uncovering these struggles allows you to create solutions in the form of a product or service, which leads to an irresistible offer and revenue.

However, we can't (and shouldn't) create solutions for every problem. That would be going one mile wide and one inch deep. On the common path to uncommon success, we go one inch wide and one mile deep. We focus on providing the best solution to our avatar's biggest struggle. Your goal is to be so good that potential competition decides it's not worth competing. That's when you know you've created something special.

But what about all the other struggles your audience will encounter along their journey? This is when it's time to create affiliate partnerships. In a nutshell, affiliate partnerships are where you recommend a product or service to your audience. If your audience decides to invest, then your affiliate partner will pay you a percentage of the sale. This is referred to as affiliate commission.

To track your leads and conversions, your affiliate partner will supply you with an *affiliate link* that will ensure you get credit for every sale made. Alternatively, your affiliate partner may create a special promo code for you to promote.

An example of this is when I urge my audience to use promo code FIRE at checkout for an additional 15 percent off. The downside to the promo code is you'll only know how many people end up buying, whereas with an affiliate link you'll also know what amount of traffic you sent to the sales page. This will allow you to see the conversion of leads into sales, which is vital because it could indicate that the sales page itself needs to be improved, which is very valuable information.

Overall, affiliate partnerships are great because they allow you to focus on delivering the solutions you should be focused on delivering, while recommending your affiliate partner's solutions to your audience's other struggles. These partnerships ensure that you'll remain the person your audience goes to for all their questions, because you can direct them to the best solution. They allow you to generate revenue both when your audience invests in your products and services, or takes your recommendations and invests with your affiliate partners.

Think about the last time your best friend called you and said, "I just watched an amazing movie last night and I know you'll love it!" You watched the movie and probably loved it because your best friend knows you and is only going to give such rave reviews when they know you're going to love it too.

That is the power of referrals when they come from trusted relationships, and you've been building these relationships on the common path to uncommon success. You've been delivering free, valuable, and consistent content to your audience. They know, like, and trust you. They admire the success you've achieved thus far.

If they're going to get advice on what solution they need to their current problem, you are the person they will look to for guidance. Creating the right affiliate partnerships allows you to become the one-stop shop for your audience. Even if you don't personally provide the solution, your recommendation will guide them in the right direction.

Once you've shown your affiliate partners that you're capable of sending highly qualified leads, it's time to take the next step. That step is to have your affiliate partner create a special landing page for you. This landing page is where your lead will be taken when they click on your affiliate link. It will have your personal branding and a special offer only for your audience. The special offer could be an extended free trial, a higher percentage discount, or additional services not typically offered.

Also, this is your chance to add value of your own to further entice your audience to invest. In the next section, I'll share how I've successfully generated over a million dollars in revenue from using the above strategies. This strategy can be time-consuming up front, but will pay big dividends over time.

You worked hard for this lead. You recommended a proven solution, so if they decide to invest, you deserve your affiliate commission.

I've seen many entrepreneurs not take this strategy seriously and miss out on countless revenue. Picture an example like this:

A member of your audience hears you talk about a great product or service you recommend and your affiliate link that will take them to the sales page. They were jogging at the time so they forgot the exact link you mentioned and instead just google the company's name and find the product on their website. If they end up buying, you will not receive your affiliate commission even though you are the reason that company made a sale. But if you follow the common path to uncommon success and are *very clear* to your audience to "use my affiliate link and you will receive an additional 15 percent off as well as an extended free trial," you better believe your audience is going to jump through hoops to make sure they find and use your affiliate link for the added features and benefits.

Remember, you earned this revenue. It's not coming out of the pockets of your audience, but of the company who you enriched by sending them a buyer. You earned it; make sure you get it!

My Affiliate Partnerships

As I write these words, affiliate revenue is responsible for approximately 50 percent of my overall revenue month over month. Besides being one of my biggest revenue streams, it's also one of my favorites. After recommending the proper product or service, I collect my commission and my work is done. There is no further training or support on my end. The lead is under the warm embrace of my affiliate and it is their job to handle all aspects of the relationship moving forward.

My most successful affiliate relationship to date is with a company called ClickFunnels (which you learned about in chapters 11 and 12). They are a company that provides all the tools you need to create a sales funnel for your business, complete with landing pages, registration forms, order forms, up-sells, down-sells, and everything in between. It's a service I use every day that has helped me generate millions in revenue over the years. Plus, I am personal friends with ClickFunnels founder and CEO, Russell Brunson, and through him I knew Click-Funnels was committed to improving the platform every day.

So, when people started to ask me how I was generating revenue, I was honest. I shared how my funnels were responsible for a significant portion of my revenue and how ClickFunnels made funnel creation easy. I then shared my affiliate link, EOFire.com/click, and urged my audience to try their fourteen-day free trial.

Over the years, I've implemented many of the strategies I talked about above.

I gave a *Freedom Journal* to every person who joined ClickFunnels through our affiliate link. Russell and I hosted a free master class on funnels that could only be accessed by joining ClickFunnels through our affiliate link. We even promoted ClickFunnels's "One Funnel Away" challenge, where everyone who signed up received a book

Russel wrote that had an entire chapter dedicated to what I would do if given thirty days to create a funnel.

Early on, I saw how ClickFunnels was going to be a valuable source of affiliate revenue. They are a *sticky* service—meaning once someone signs up for ClickFunnels and begins to build their funnels, landing pages, order forms, and checkout pages on the software, it's going to take an act of God for that individual to switch to another service.

The time, energy, and bandwidth it takes to learn a software is significant, and once we get comfortable with a specific service, we resist change. ClickFunnels is a perfect example of this truism. When my audience signed up for ClickFunnels, they stayed with ClickFunnels.

The benefit for me? Month over month, year over year, I am generating revenue every time my affiliate's monthly bill is paid. To date, that revenue has added up to over $1,350,000. That is money in my pocket for recommending a great service.

Once I saw how lucrative my partnership with ClickFunnels was, I began to create more ways to recommend my audience to their service. I offered them a discount to sponsor my podcast, with the caveat that I would be able to promote my affiliate link in return for the sponsorship discount.

I created a free course where I taught my audience how to create a funnel that converts. After completing *Funnel on Fire*, I recommend ClickFunnels's free fourteen-day trial as the next logical step for those wanting to create their funnel on fire. This strategy allowed me to create massive value for free, then recommend a free trial to a great service, and let ClickFunnels do what they do best and convert free trials into long-term customers and evangelists.

I also promote ClickFunnels in my email welcome sequence and on the resources page at EOFire.com/resources. Basically, wherever it makes sense to recommend a great company that provides an amazing solution for my audience's major struggles, I do it because it's a win, win, win: A win for my audience because they get the best solution to their problem. A win for my affiliate because they get a paying customer. And a win for me because I get to add more value to my audience's life and earn an affiliate commission in the process.

I hope this example sparks both excitement and ideas for you. You don't have to be everything to everyone. You can focus on what you do best and promote other companies' products and services in the areas in which they excel, creating that win, win, win for all parties involved.

You got this!

An Entrepreneur on Fire's Path to Uncommon Success

JILL AND JOSH STANTON ON CREATING AND MANAGING AFFILIATE PARTNERSHIPS

Affiliate marketing has made businesses millions and ordinary people millionaires. —BO BENNET

THE YEAR WAS 2011. Jill and Josh Stanton decided it was time to screw the nine to five. They vowed to never get a "real job" again and set off in search of the best way to attain financial and lifestyle freedom.

After some research online, they decided their best bet to achieve their goals was affiliate marketing. They loved how the affiliate model would allow them to refer people to the products and services they were looking for in return for a percentage of the sale while having nothing to do with fulfillment. This type of business would allow them to fulfill their dreams of traveling overseas while not being tied to a time zone or boss.

Skin care was their first foray into affiliate marketing, because their market research revealed a lot of people were buying skin care products online. Jill and Josh weren't sure where to start, so they began creating content around skin care. They requested samples of skin care products, which they used for video reviews on their website.

Over time, organic traffic began to roll in as Google saw people were getting the answers they needed for specific skin care-related queries.

The articles contained affiliate links, and the commissions ranged from 5 percent all the way to 50 percent. They continued to crank out blog posts, video reviews, and guest posts.

At the end of the first month they had made $1,100 in commissions. Jill and Josh were fired up and set a BHAG (Big Hairy Audacious Goal) of making $5,000 a month on the regular. This amount would allow them to realize their dream of becoming digital nomads in Asia.

A few months later, they hit their $5,000 goal and celebrated in style with a bottle of wine on a lake in Toronto. They loved how the money kept rolling in and that they weren't on the hook for any product delivery, customer support, or fulfillment of any kind. They decided it was time to diversify and added makeup, hair, personal hygiene, weight loss, supplements, and a few other niches to their affiliate marketing machine.

They made the leap to Thailand and continued to rinse and repeat their affiliate model, upping their revenue to $13,000 a month. Most days, Jill and Josh were working between two and three hours and enjoying life to the fullest. They launched ScrewTheNineToFive.com as a lifestyle blog with the goal of telling their story and helping others achieve the financial success they had found.

ScrewTheNineToFive.com struggled to gain traction until Jill and Josh started teaching what they knew, affiliate marketing. To date, they've helped hundreds of entrepreneurs successfully launch their affiliate marketing businesses in a wide variety of niches while continuing to crush it in the affiliate space.

In one year's time (August 2019 to August 2020), they generated $890,000 in commissions. Jill and Josh have these three tips when it comes to affiliate marketing.

1. Make a list of potential products that are in your niche that you can review and add to your website and social media.

2. Make a list of the products and programs that you use and create tutorials on how to maximize their value. A great example of this is ScreenFlow. I wanted to learn more about ScreenFlow before I purchased it so I took a free tutorial I found online. When I decided to purchase ScreenFlow, I used the affiliate link of the creator of the tutorial. If you can work a deal with the company who is offering the product to provide your audience an added discount or bonus, you will increase your conversions exponentially.

3. Are there courses or communities that you are not an expert in that you can direct your audience to? Focus on the one thing you are best at and connect your audience with the solutions they need in all the other areas.

In Jill's words: "Affiliate marketing is connecting our audience with the people, products, programs, and tools we use, like, and believe in. Trust is the currency in affiliate marketing."

Thank you, Jill and Josh Stanton.

You can learn more about Jill and Josh at ScrewTheNineToFive.com.

Check out your free companion course for added support along *The Common Path to Uncommon Success*: EOFire.com/success-course.

CHAPTER 17

Keep the Money You Make

It's not how much money you make, but how much money you keep, how hard it works for you, and how many generations you keep it for.
—ROBERT KIYOSAKI

T ruer words have never been spoken. Remember how I started this book with the words "You've been lied to"? It's happening every day, and the most damaging lies are the ones people tell about the money they are making. Some people are outright lying so they can "fake it till they make it." Others are massaging their words to make it sound like they are crushing it while they are just scraping by.

Social media is littered with claims such as *I just had a six-figure launch! My business crossed the million-dollar mark for the year! I'm making five figures a week!*

Some of those statements are outright lies and others, while technically true, are just as deceiving. It's not hard to have a $100,000 launch when you spend $200,000. It's not hard to generate $15,000 in a week when your payroll and ad spend is $20,000. It's not hard to generate a million dollars in sales on Amazon when your actual profit margin is 1 percent for twelve months of *hard work* (these are real numbers from a past guest of mine).

I have many friends who work *very* hard, bring so much value to the world, generate a *lot* of revenue from their efforts, but at the end of the year are left wondering, where's all that money I made?

I'll tell you where it went. Ad spend, payroll, and above all else, taxes. Those big three will eat away at your profit every second you're not focused on keeping the money you make.

Entrepreneurs love pointing to Amazon never turning a profit and how Jeff Bezos is one of the richest people in the world. My response? Good luck creating the next Amazon.

The common path to uncommon success is not about creating the next Amazon. It's about creating a life of financial freedom and fulfillment. It's about creating a business that lights you up every day. It's about creating a business that adds massive value to the world in your area of expertise. It's about creating a business that allows you to live the life you want, beholden to no one.

It took time, but I have turned *Entrepreneurs on Fire* into that business. I'm able to travel on a whim. I spend over ninety days a year on vacation. Every morning I wake up in my dream home in Puerto Rico, and my calendar only contains the appointments and activities I chose. I receive emails by the hundreds from my audience sharing how one of my interviews, books, videos, or posts sparked something inside and set them on their path toward uncommon success.

That is my fuel. That is my fire. That is what I want for you.

But none of the above can happen until you start to keep the money you make. As humans, we LOVE to live right up to our means. If you make $40,000 a year, you squeak by on $40,000 a year.

When you get a raise to $60,000, you think all your troubles are over. *An extra $20,000! I'm rich!* Then a year goes by and you might have a few more "things," but financially you're in the exact same boat as when you made $40,000. That boat being empty of everything but possibly $400 in emergency savings.

Did you know 40 percent of Americans can't cover a $400 emergency expense? That information came straight from the Federal Reserve Board. What a scary statistic. When you are living paycheck to paycheck, there's a stress that will always be present. The first accident, blip in the economy, or unforeseen expense could cause the house of cards to topple. It feels like disaster is right around the corner, and it is.

But those who can survive a downturn will be very well positioned to thrive when the storm abates. Another problem with living at your means is the inability to invest in your business. Without excess capital, you can't grow your team, dedicate money to ad spend, and improve your businesses infrastructure. If you're in an industry where your competitors are doing these things, you'll be left behind.

But there is good news. If you commit to keeping the money you make and build a financial war chest, you'll be able to deploy your assets in ways that will fortify and grow your business.

There are two amazing books that will further expound upon this topic as well as provide specific tactics you can employ. The first book is a classic: *The Richest Man in Babylon*, by George S. Clason. You'll be taken back thousands of years to learn a timeless principle: pay yourself first. Once you've acquired the habit of paying yourself at least ten cents for every dollar you make, you'll be on your way to growing a financial war chest. Once you have a financial war chest, you can make your money work for *you*. It's a powerful concept and one that has always stuck with me.

The second book is very tactical and strategic: *Profit First*, by Mike Michalowicz. Mike is a financial genius and I personally know of dozens of struggling businesses who have turned their financials around by implementing the strategies in *Profit First*.

The common path to uncommon success is about creating financial freedom and fulfillment. You can't do that with an empty bank account. You can't do that without keeping the money you make.

Learn the principles in these books and you will be on your way to uncommon success.

You got this!

Keeping the Money I Made

The year was 2015. The location, San Diego, California. I was halfway through the second year in a row where I would gross well over $2 million. That was exiting. What wasn't exciting was that I had just written my quarterly tax check to Uncle Sam for $250,000.

I knew when that check cleared, I would have less than $750,000 in the bank. How was this possible? I had made over $2 million in 2014 and was on pace to cross $4 million in 2015. Where was all my money?

I decided it was time to get serious about my finances. For the first couple years, I was just happy to keep the lights on. Now, I had big financial aspirations.

My accountant and I sat down, did a full audit, and the results were not pretty. With my ad spend, payroll, and, worst of all, taxes, I was keeping less than 25 percent of the money I made. That's not a terrible percentage for most businesses, but it was not the percentage I wanted to see with *Entrepreneurs on Fire*.

From day one, my goal with *Entrepreneurs on Fire* was to run a lean, mean, profit-making machine. I wanted financial freedom and fulfillment. I wanted to keep the money I was making.

My accountant said the following words that cut me to the core. "John, it's not hard to make money in California, but it's near impossible to become wealthy." Those words stung. I was making money in California, that was for sure, but after ad spend, payroll, and the 51 percent state and federal tax I was paying, there was not a lot left over. It seemed the more money I made, the smaller percentage I kept.

It was incredibly demoralizing. I found myself losing interest in taking on new projects. It was not a great time in my business career.

I began to dedicate my time to looking for legal ways to lower my tax rate, but everything seemed so complicated and confusing. Then,

I read about Puerto Rico, a commonwealth of the US that was incentivizing mainland entrepreneurs to move to their Caribbean island with something called Act 20.

In a nutshell, Act 20 would take my effective tax rate from 51 percent to 4 percent. I knew it was too good to be true, but after my CPA vetted the Act and I chatted with a few people who had made the move, I knew it was the right time and opportunity.

On May 1, 2016, Kate and I moved to Puerto Rico, found our dream home, and have been here ever since. We keep our team lean, our expenses low, and keep (almost) all the money we make.

Since 2013, we've been publishing a monthly income report where we share our revenue generated and expenses incurred. We expound upon the successes and failures we had over the past month and bring our CPA in to provide a tax tip and our lawyer to provide a legal tip. Our income reports help us maintain our pledge of being open, honest, and transparent with our audience.

We still have months where our expenses get a little high, but our income reports ensure we have a finger on the pulse of our business—our profits. If you want to keep sharing your voice, message, and mission with the world, you need to prioritize your profits. You can't make an impact if you can't support yourself and your loved ones.

You're on the common path to uncommon success. We're here to make an impact and create a life of financial freedom and fulfillment.

You got this!

An Entrepreneur on Fire's Path to Uncommon Success

RAMIT SETHI ON KEEPING THE MONEY YOU MAKE

**There is a gigantic difference between
earning a great deal of money and being rich.**
—MARLENE DIETRICH

WE ALL KNOW what it's like to play defense with our money. You get to the end of the month, look at your bills, shrug, and say, "I guess I spent that much." We try to get one step ahead financially, but an "unexpected expense" always derails our plans. This is what happens when you play defense with your money.

Playing offense is an entirely different game. It allows us to dream bigger. To take that vacation and fly business class. To eat at that fancy restaurant without having to skip appetizers.

Playing offense allows us to use our money to live a rich life.

When Ramit started writing about money at IWillTeachYouToBeRich. com, he was in his early twenties, single, and already saving for his wedding day. Ramit was years away from meeting his wife, but when it happened, he wanted to be financially prepared to afford a beautiful wedding.

Years later, while on a book tour in Portland, Oregon, a young woman thanked him for the inspiration to start saving for her wedding before she was even engaged. When Ramit asked her to tell her story on a quick video to share how proactive she was being, she declined, claiming "it would be weird to talk about" because she was not even engaged yet.

Ramit asked himself, "Why is it so weird to plan for things that we know are going to happen?" Most people will get married. Most people will have children, buy a car and a house. Most people will eventually retire and have elderly parents to care for. Why was it weird to plan and save for these likely life events?

What if, instead of playing defense our entire lives, we played offense? What if we dreamed bigger? What if, instead of only thinking about what we need to do with our money, we thought about what we wanted to do?

Playing offense means spending money on things you love while cutting spending mercilessly on things that are not important to you. Ramit recommends a ten-year savings strategy. Start an automatic savings account and set up monthly investments. Now you can plan further ahead and plan your dreams.

Over the next ten years, what are the *big* purchases you want to make? This can be a fun activity you do with your partner. Kids? Childcare? Travel? Where and for how long?

When you write down your dreams, it allows you to start small because you have plenty of time to reach your financial goals. Starting now makes these dreams possible. In Ramit's own words: "Take money from a place of playing defense, from a source of anxiety and nervousness and guilt, and reframe it into playing offense. Create automatic systems and focus on how you can use money to live your version of a rich life."

Thank you, Ramit Sethi.

You can learn more about Ramit at IWillTeachYouToBeRich.com.

Check out your free companion course for added
support along *The Common Path to Uncommon Success*:
EOFire.com/success-course.

CHAPTER 18

The Well of Knowledge

A ship in the harbor is safe,
but that is not what ships are built for.
—JOHN A. SHEDD

What a journey we've been on. Now it's time to take your ship out to sea. It's time to join us on the common path to uncommon success. This final chapter is called "The Well of Knowledge" for a reason. It's a compilation of the best advice I've received over the years with my thoughts added. My hope is that you'll visit "The Well of Knowledge" every time you need a dose of inspiration, motivation, and guidance.

Enjoy!

My Well of Knowledge

This first section will be "JLDisms." These are my favorite truisms that I've seen proven time and again over the course of the 2,500+ interviews I've conducted with successful entrepreneurs since 2012.

FOCUS: Follow One Course Until Success

This may be my most uttered phrase on an *Entrepreneurs on Fire* interview. I love how it's a perfect acronym: Follow One Course Until Success. Whenever you feel overwhelmed, or too busy, or too stressed out on your journey, it's time to find one single focus and cut out all the other noise.

For me, it was hosting one more quality interview for *Entrepreneurs on Fire*. That was the one course that would lead me to success. Everything else was a nice-to-have, but wasn't my driving FOCUS.

Successful entrepreneurs know exactly what their one course to success is. Do you?

Looking for permission? Check the mirror.

Time and again, I see people looking to others for permission. Permission to start, permission to stop, permission to breathe. Why do we feel the need to seek permission from others?

On the common path to uncommon success, the only permission you need is from yourself. This is your life, your opportunity, your path. Why should we allow someone else to lead the way?

In a single word, *don't*.

Compare and despair.

Comparing yourself to others will always lead to despair. There will always be someone richer, taller, skinnier, more muscular, prettier, happier, more successful. There will also always be someone poorer, fatter, weaker, uglier, sadder, and less successful.

If you remember the following, you'll lead a happier life: *The only person you should compare yourself to is you, yesterday.* If you're winning that comparison *most* of the time, you're winning at life.

On the common path to uncommon success, we win at life.

Get traction and hang on for dear life.

One of the hardest things to attain as an entrepreneur is proof of concept. When you've created a solution that people are willing to pay for, it's time to slam your foot on the gas.

I've seen countless entrepreneurs reach the proof of concept stage and then inexplicably shift into coasting mode. Big mistake. When you get traction, go all in and hang on for your life.

I've always loved the saying *make hay while the sun is shining*. Farmers know the time to harvest hay is when the sun is shining, because there's always a storm around the corner.

In 2013, live webinars were crushing it for us when it came to making sales for Podcasters' Paradise. I slammed my foot on the gas and did a live webinar every week for three years. I knew the sun would stop shining at some point, and I made sure to squeeze every drop of opportunity out of live webinars before the storm clouds moved in.

You got this!

Live below your means.

Why are 60 percent of Americans unable to write an unexpected $400 check? Because we've become a society trained to live right up to our paycheck. Did you just get a raise from $60,000 to $80,000? Congratulations!

Are you curious why your bank account still looks the same at the end of the year? Because you adjusted your lifestyle to $80,000 a year. Yes, you may have a few more things in your garage and an extra trip you enjoyed, but you're condemning your future self to a life lacking financial freedom and fulfillment.

Successful entrepreneurs live below their means. They build up their financial war chest and use it to:

- Invest in their business
- Invest in other businesses

- Make it through the rainy days, weeks, or even months that are ahead.

You are on the path to financial freedom and fulfillment—make it count.

Get 1 percent better every day.

Overnight success is a myth. Getting 1 percent better every day is not only attainable but it's the surest way to success. When you improve each day by 1 percent, over time your progress is astronomical thanks to the compound effect.

Two books worth bringing up are: *The Slight Edge* by Jeff Olsen and *The Compound Effect* by Darren Hardy. These books share the value of getting 1 percent better every day. Hold yourself accountable to this measurement and you'll be well on your way to financial freedom and fulfillment.

Put in the reps.

There's a question that baffles me above all others. Why do people think they could/should be good at something they've never done before? Every day I get an email where a person is claiming they can't do X because they've never done X and are not good at X.

My response is always the same. *Why do you expect to be good at something you've never done before?*

Was Michael Jordan a great basketball player before he dribbled a ball? Was Phil Mickelson a great golfer before he swung a club? *Of course not.* Everyone who's become great at something has *put in the reps.*

I've been asked when I considered myself a good podcaster. My answer? Four hundred eighty episodes. That is a year and a half of waking up every day and putting in the reps. Getting a little better at my craft every week.

Do you want to become great at something? Awesome! Here's the single ingredient: put in the reps.

Be consistent.

Entrepreneurs don't fail. They just stop doing the things that would eventually make them successful.

Publishing a hundred podcast episodes is a lot of work. But when I reached a hundred episodes, I was not successful. Not even close. It took thirteen months of daily podcasting to break through financially. That's over four hundred episodes. I had to stay consistent four times longer than the hundred-episode milestone to find success, and once I found it, I had to remain consistent to hold onto the success I had achieved.

Entrepreneurs who achieve financial freedom and fulfillment aren't better, or luckier, or smarter than others, they've just been at it longer. Woody Allen was right when he said *80 percent of success is showing up*. Are you willing to commit to show up? Not just today, not just tomorrow, but over the long haul?

My common path to uncommon success included showing up two thousand days in a row with two thousand episodes. That's five-and-a-half years of releasing an interview *every day*. What is your commitment?

You got this!

You only need to be right once.

For the first thirty-two years of my life, I was wrong about a lot of things. But at thirty-two, I was right one time about one thing: the need for a daily podcast interviewing successful entrepreneurs. That one thing led me to the financial freedom and fulfillment I now enjoy.

Since the age of thirty-two, I've been wrong about many things, but that single idea was all I needed. Take courage and have faith. Walk up to the plate and take a swing, and then keep on swinging. You can miss that ball a thousand times, but on that next pitch, you just might identify the idea that allows you to hit a grand slam.

Thomas Edison shared a great quote when he was trying to figure out how to perfect the light bulb: *I have not failed. I've just found ten thousand ways that won't work.* The 10,001st way worked for Thomas

Edison, and look where we are now. To achieve financial freedom and fulfillment, we only need to be right once.

You got this!

All the magic happens outside of your comfort zone.

We love living in our comfort zone. It's so gosh dang comfortable. However, all the magic happens outside of your comfort zone.

It's scary to push yourself to new limits, to take risks and chase your dreams. But that's the path to uncommon success. Join me on this path; I got your back!

Figure out what sets you on fire and have tunnel vision.

What sets you on fire? What lights you up? What gives you those goose bumps of energy and makes you feel alive? Once you identify your zone of fire, have tunnel vision to create the best solution to a real problem.

When you are willing to eat, live, and breathe your zone of fire with complete tunnel vision, the universe will align and you'll find your way to financial freedom and fulfillment.

You got this!

The Well of Knowledge, Variety Edition

I need to give a huge tip of the cap to James Clear and his incredible book, *Atomic Habits*, as well as his must-read email newsletter, which you can subscribe to at JamesClear.com. Below are value bombs from a variety of individuals that James brought to my attention via his newsletter and book. After this section, I have an entire section featuring James Clear(isms) you will *not* want to miss!

If you don't get what you want,
it's a sign either that you did not seriously want it,
or that you tried to bargain over the price.
—RUDYARD KIPLING

Achieving financial freedom and fulfillment is tough. The price is hard work, consistency, and patience. If you don't really want it, you'll try to bargain over the price tag and that's a recipe for disaster.

The common path will help you achieve uncommon success because we focus on the ingredients you need to succeed.

Trust the process.

Courage doesn't always roar.
Sometimes courage is a quiet voice at the end
of the day saying, "I will try again tomorrow."
—MARY ANNE RADMACHER

We've all seen those individuals full of fire and brimstone, seemingly overflowing with confidence and courage. Within months, most have faded into oblivion.

On the common path to uncommon success, courage is simply saying "I did my best today; I will try again tomorrow."

Whatever you are not changing, you are choosing.
—LAURIE BUCHANAN

We make choices every day. Some choose to stay the same, to stay stagnant, to stay put. On the common path to uncommon success, we choose to evolve, adjust, and adapt with the world around us. We choose to ask our audience what they need and provide the ever-changing solution. We choose financial freedom and fulfilment.

When one teaches, two learn.
—ROBERT HEINLEIN

You have knowledge to share with the world. When you share that knowledge, not only are you teaching others but you are learning as well. You're learning how to teach, how to solve the struggles of your student, and how to apply your knowledge to impact the world. You're learning the common path to uncommon success and setting the world on fire!

People do not decide their futures, they decide their habits and their habits decide their futures.
—F. M. ALEXANDER

Many people claim they want financial freedom and fulfillment above all else, but their habits don't reflect their desire. Those who achieve financial freedom and fulfillment first identify the habits that will lead to uncommon success and implement those habits daily. Your daily habits are your building blocks to uncommon success: identify, implement, execute.

You got this!

Sometimes magic is just someone spending more time on something than anyone else might reasonably expect.
—PENN & TELLER

Are you willing to put in the reps? Are you willing to work at something ten times longer than your closest competition? Are you willing to work so hard that your solution is the best solution by a country mile? When you put in more reps than anyone else might reasonably expect, you create magic.

Let's create magic!

> The person who asks is a fool for five minutes,
> but the person who does not ask remains a fool forever.
> —PROVERB

Those on the common path to uncommon success never stop learning. I will always have a mentor. I will always be a part of a mastermind. I know the power of not being the smartest person in the room. Do you?

> Not one of your pertinent ancestors was squashed,
> devoured, drowned, starved, stranded, stuck fast, untimely
> wounded, or otherwise deflected from its life's quest of
> delivering a tiny charge of genetic material to the right partner
> at the right moment in order to perpetuate the only possible
> sequence of hereditary combinations that could result—
> eventually, astoundingly, and all too briefly—in you.
> —BILL BRYSON

Perspective is hard to attain and even harder to hold onto. As mortar rounds were dropping around me during my tour of duty in the Iraqi war, I remember so clearly thinking, *If I make it home safe, I will never take another day of freedom for granted.* Since then, I've taken *many* days of freedom for granted, but I try hard to maintain a perspective of gratitude. No matter how bad my day might be, nothing will compare to that horrific day in Iraq.

What can you use in your past to help remind you of how good you have it today? Perspective is a powerful weapon—wield it wisely.

How to Get Better at Sales

1. Sales is a lot like golf. You can make it so complicated as to be impossible or you can simply walk up and hit the ball. I've been leading and building sales orgs for almost twenty years and my advice is to walk up and hit the ball.

2. Sales is about people and it's about problem-solving. It is not about solutions or technology or chemicals or lines of code or artichokes. It's about people and it's about solving problems.

3. People buy four things and four things only. Ever. Those four things are time, money, sex, and approval/peace of mind. If you try selling something other than those four things you will fail.

4. People buy aspirin always. They buy vitamins only occasionally and at unpredictable times. Sell aspirin.

5. I say in every talk I give: "All things being equal, people buy from their friends. So, make everything else equal, then go make a lot of friends."

6. Being valuable and useful is all you ever need to do to sell things. Help people out. Send interesting posts. Write birthday cards. Record videos sharing your ideas for growing their business. Introduce people who would benefit from knowing each other, then get out of the way, expecting nothing in return. Do this consistently and authentically and people will find ways to give you money. I promise.

7. No one cares about your quota, your payroll, your opex, your burn rate, etc. No one. They care about the problem you are solving for them.

There is more than 100 trillion dollars in the global economy just waiting for you to breathe it in.

Good luck.

—Colin Dowling

I can't improve upon the above, so I won't try.

The Well of Knowledge, James Clear Edition

James Clear is an entrepreneur I look up to for many reasons. He's worked incredibly hard at his craft of writing. He's been very consistent and patient over the years, which paid off *big* with his *New York Times* bestselling book, *Atomic Habits*. His newsletter is the only must-read newsletter that arrives in my inbox weekly and you can learn more at JamesClear.com.

Below are my favorite James Clear quotes over the last few years. Enjoy!

* * *

Be forgiving with your past self. Be strict with your present self. Be flexible with your future self.

We can't change the past, only learn from it. We have total control of this moment in time. Take the wheel and drive! The world is ever evolving, as is your future. Don't be too strict on a future that has yet to unfold. Allow yourself the space to adjust and thrive.

* * *

Wealth is the power to choose. Financial wealth is the power to choose how to spend money. Social wealth is the power to choose who to hang out with. Time wealth is the power to choose how to spend your day. Mental wealth is the power to choose how to spend your attention.

The goal of the common path to uncommon success is to provide you the power of choice. When you can choose how to spend your money, time, and energy, you have truly achieved uncommon success.

* * *

If you want to take something more seriously, do it publicly. Publishing an article pressures you to think clearly. Competing in a race pressures you to train consistently. Presenting on any topic pressures you to learn it. Social pressure forces you to up your game.

Accountability is everything. It's why I'm committed to being in a mastermind filled with those I know, like, and trust. We will always do better when we are being held accountable by those we respect. Make it real. Up your game. Uncommon success is *outside* your comfort zone, so go get it!

* * *

Most failures are one-time costs. Most regrets are recurring costs. The pain of inaction stings longer than the pain of incorrect action.

Those who take the most swings hit the most home runs. It allows us to learn from our failure, adjust, and swing again. Remember, regret is one thing you do not want in excess at the end of your life. Release regret when you embrace *action*!

* * *

Needless commitments are more wasteful than needless possessions. Possessions can be ignored, but commitments are a recurring debt that must be paid for with your time and attention. You can create a lot of meaning in your own life by helping someone else do something that is meaningful to them.

For a long time, I said *yes* to everything. Then I realized that each time I said yes to one thing, I was saying no to everything else I otherwise could be doing with that time. Since that revelation, I've been *very* careful with my commitments.

The common path to uncommon success is about freedom, not confinement.

* * *

Every action is a vote for the type of person you wish to become.

Did you just eat a bag of Oreos? That's a vote for becoming a fat person. Did you work out for five days in a row? That's a vote for becoming a person with optimal health. How are you voting with your actions?

* * *

The way to attract good luck is to be reliable in a valuable area. The more you repeatedly deliver value, the more people seek you out for that value. Your reputation is a magnet. Once you become known for something, relevant opportunities come to you with no extra work.

When you refuse to niche into an underserved market, you're relegating yourself to a life of obscurity. No one wants advice from the 10,634th most successful person on Instagram. They want to talk to the most successful person who trains deaf dogs to play piano. I know that's a random niche, but you get the idea. Become the best in your niche and people will seek you out and opportunities will be everywhere. Period.

* * *

In a world where information is abundant and easy to access, the real advantage is knowing where to focus.

Laser focus is what the common path to uncommon success is all about. What can you focus on that is not already easy and abundant to access in today's world? What problem can you solve that can't be solved with a few keystrokes on Google? Financial freedom and fulfillment are yours when you discover the answer.

* * *

The best way to get the attention and respect of exceptional people is to do exceptional work. Like attracts like.

Put in the reps. Get a little bit better every day. One morning, you'll wake up and be exceptional and people will beat down a path to your door.

You got this!

* * *

Not taking things personally is a superpower.

I remember my first negative review so clearly. It was like a punch to the gut. I mentioned it to my mentor and her response was, *You've finally arrived!* She explained that everyone who creates something meaningful in this world is taking a stance, and whenever you take a stance, you'll have haters. Haters might disagree with you, or dislike you, or more likely are just having a bad day.

If you remember this one mantra, getting over negative comments will be much easier. *Hurt people hurt people.* So simple, yet so true. Haters are hurting inside. There's something broken inside and they're lashing out at others. Feel empathy toward your haters. They may not deserve it, but they need it.

* * *

Creative ideas happen when you stop thinking about what others will think.

Why are you willing to work so hard for financial freedom and fulfillment? Is it for your neighbor? Is it for your high school friend? Didn't think so.

It's for you and your loved ones. Uncommon success comes from creative ideas. Creative ideas come when you stop caring about what others think.

* * *

The more control you have over your attention, the more control you have over your future.

Everything that exists in this world is meant to distract you. People are paid millions of dollars to distract you. Everyone is screaming for your attention. If you want to achieve financial freedom and fulfillment, *control your attention.* Once you control your attention and focus on the common path, financial freedom and fulfillment are yours.

* * *

Knowledge is the compound interest of curiosity.

Coming up with your big idea is not easy. One of the key components is curiosity. If you can compound your curiosity by obsessing over a topic, your knowledge will grow and mastery will form.

Mastery will lead to you becoming the master of your niche. Becoming the master of your niche will lead to uncommon success.

* * *

If you have good habits, time becomes your ally. All you need is patience.

When you identify and implement the right habits, it's only a matter of time before you find your way to financial freedom and fulfillment. Make time work for you, not the other way around.

* * *

The Paradox of Freedom: The way to expand your freedom is to narrow your focus. Stay focused on saving to achieve financial freedom. Stay focused on training to achieve physical freedom. Stay focused on learning to achieve intellectual freedom.

All I'll add to the above is this: There's a reason why *focus* is my favorite word. Follow one course until success.

* * *

Where you spend your attention is where you spend your life.

We have one life to live. Find your passion, combine it with value you can provide the world, and give it your full attention. Then you'll spend your life doing what you love and impacting the lives of others. If that's not the definition of fulfillment, what is?

* * *

Stop worrying about how long it will take and get started. Time will pass either way.

We're human beings. We love to procrastinate. We love to procrastinate about procrastination. If I could scream one thing from the rooftops it would be: *Start now! No, not in ten seconds. Now!*

* * *

Without hard work, a great strategy remains a dream. Without a great strategy, hard work becomes a nightmare.

If you want to achieve financial freedom and fulfillment, work hard. But your hard work must have a purpose. This is where strategy comes in. If you're running one million miles an hour in the wrong direction, you'll end up a million miles from where you need to be.

Work hard. Work smart. Have a sound strategy. Execute.

* * *

The most useful form of patience is persistence. Patience implies waiting for things to improve on their own. Persistence implies keeping your head down and continuing to work when things take longer than you expect.

Each day is a new battle to say yes to what matters and say no to what doesn't. Focus is a practice.

Slow and steady often wins because it keeps you motivated. Take on manageable challenges and you'll get frequent signals of progress. Bite off more than you can chew and progress stalls. When you make progress, you want to keep going. When you break progress, you want to stop.

Don't break progress. Don't stop. Each day is a new battle to say yes to. You got this!

The Well of Knowledge, Kevin Kelly Edition

These value bombs come from Kevin Kelly, who published *68 Bits of Unsolicited Advice* on his sixty-eighth birthday. You can find out more about Kevin at KK.org or google "Kevin Kelly 68" for this article.

Below are my fourteen favorite bits of unsolicited advice from Kevin's article.

Enjoy!

* * *

Learn how to learn from those you disagree with, or even offend you. See if you can find the truth in what they believe.

If we miss opportunities to learn from every situation, we limit the knowledge we can gain. Every situation in life is packed with opportunities to learn. If we learn from those whom we disagree with or are offended by, we're taking advantage of growing our knowledge in ways that will serve us well.

Common success comes from shutting ourselves off from learning opportunities. Uncommon success is the result of learning from all.

* * *

Being enthusiastic is worth 25 IQ points.

When I launched *Entrepreneurs on Fire*, I was *not* a good podcast host. I was nervous, inexperienced, and raw. But I was enthusiastic. Very enthusiastic. At times, too enthusiastic. But my enthusiasm was infectious. It put my guests at ease and got my listeners fired up. They knew I cared. They knew I was working hard to improve. They knew I was doing my best.

At the end of the day, we root for people who are doing their best. Be enthusiastic about what you do. What's the alternative?

* * *

Always demand a deadline. A deadline weeds out the extraneous and the ordinary. It prevents you from trying to make it perfect, so you have to make it different. Different is better.

I want to begin with the end. *Different is better.* Now back to the beginning. Deadlines are everything.

Parkinson's law states that *tasks will expand to the time allotted.* Those words are 100 percent true. If you give yourself all day to accomplish one task, it will take you all day. When I started my day with an open calendar and plenty of time to write, it was overwhelming and I continued to procrastinate. But when I made the simple switch of setting a timer for forty-two minutes and pressing *start*, suddenly it was manageable.

I was in a race to write as many quality words as I could in forty-two minutes. I knew at the end of the forty-two minutes I would have a break and get to do something enjoyable for my eighteen minutes of "refresh" time.

We must always set deadlines. Once that deadline hits, we ship. Uncommon success does not derive from perfection but rather from imperfect action.

You got this!

* * *

Don't be afraid to ask a question that may sound stupid because 99 percent of the time everyone else is thinking of the same question and is too embarrassed to ask it.

This reminds me of a passage I read about Henry Ford. He was on trial in a court of law and the lawyers were trying to make him out to be stupid by asking him a series of trivia questions. Ford answered, "I don't know" to almost every one of them. The lawyers got flabbergasted and asked how such an "unlearned man" could run the most successful motor company in the world, Ford Motors.

Henry responded with a version of "Because I know what I need to know to run the most successful motor company in the world, and anything else is just clutter in my head. If I ever need to know something, I have one of my assistants look it up in a book."

My reason for sharing this story is that it's foolish to think we need to know everything. We need to learn the knowledge that will guide us on our specific quest for uncommon success. For everything else, there's Google. Next time you have a question and feel silly about asking it, ask anyway. It shows you have the intelligence to learn from others and the confidence not to be embarrassed by it.

* * *

Gratitude will unlock all other virtues and is something you can get better at.

I start each day by completing the following sentence, *I am grateful for* . . .

Gratitude is the core foundation of everything. The more we can live in a mindset of gratitude, the more we will enjoy our time in this world. I find myself slipping out of gratitude even when I have the best of intentions not to, but as Kevin Kelly says, gratitude is something you can get better at. As we improve in our gratitude, everything else in our life benefits as a result.

* * *

Pros are just amateurs who know how to gracefully recover from their mistakes.

We're all amateurs. As much as we like to fool ourselves, we're just a bunch of kids running around on a rock in the middle of a massive universe trying to figure it out. Pros are the ones who make the same mistakes we all do, but recover so gracefully that we don't notice their mistake or are in awe at how they salvaged the situation.

Become great at making mistakes and even greater at recovering from them.

* * *

Don't be the best. Be the only.

Being the best at anything is a daunting task. If you told me to become the best at X, I would study those who are considered at the top of their field at X and immediately feel overwhelmed and hopeless.

That's how I felt at the beginning of my podcasting journey. I studied those who were considered at the top of the podcasting world and knew I could never compete. They were so experienced, knowledgeable, and just plain good.

Then, I explored the unexplored world within podcasting. That was what led me to become the only. I launched the first daily podcast interviewing the world's most successful entrepreneurs. I was not good, but I was the only.

Being the only was enough to achieve uncommon success.

*   *   *

Don't take it personally when someone turns you down. Assume they are like you: busy, occupied, distracted. Try again later. It's amazing how often a second try works.

I have been on both sides of this equation many times. When I first launched *Entrepreneurs on Fire*, I would get discouraged when people turned down my interview request. However, I found that if I followed up courteously two or three months later, I often got a yes, as the timing was simply better.

Currently, I get bombarded by opportunities. Some days I feel overwhelmed and simply say no to everything. Other days I take the time to evaluate each opportunity and say yes to the most promising.

Take nothing personally. People are living their own crazy, busy, and distracting lives. Every *no* should be considered a *not now*.

Always act with respect and courtesy in every situation and you'll find opportunities will bloom on the second or third try.

You got this!

*   *   *

The purpose of a habit is to remove that action from self-negotiation. You no longer expend energy deciding whether to do it. You just do it. Good habits can range from telling the truth, to flossing.

Once you ingrain an action in your life, whether it be positive or negative, it begins to work for you or against you. Habits are powerful building blocks, which is why we want to stack good habits wherever possible. Good habits form the foundation that is critical to achieving the financial freedom and fulfillment we desire.

Start stacking.

*   *   *

The more you are interested in others, the more interesting they find you. To be interesting, be interested.

Do you have those friends who just talk, talk, and talk? They are not interested in anything you say or do, they just talk. Over time, we discover ourselves finding them less and less interesting. If you want people to find you interesting, be interested in them. Ask them questions. Be curious about their activities. Care about their lives.

A magical thing will happen: they'll want to learn more about you, because, suddenly, they find you quite fascinating.

*   *   *

To make something good, just do it. To make something great, just re-do it, re-do it, re-do it. The secret to making fine things is in re-making them.

Wake up in the morning. Put in the reps. Go to bed.

Wake up in the morning. Put in the reps. Go to bed.

That is how you become great.

I read a study about a pottery class that fits so well here. The teacher divided the room in two. Half of the room would be graded only on their single best piece of pottery for the entire semester. One piece of pottery, one grade. The better the piece of pottery, the higher the grade.

The other half of the room would only be graded on quantity. The more pieces of pottery they made, the higher the grade. The quality did not matter in the least. By the end of the semester, a funny thing happened.

The students who were being graded on quality had spent all their time trying to make the perfect piece of pottery and as a result made very few over the entire semester, and they were all poor quality. The students who were being graded on quantity had piles and piles of crappy pots, but something funny happened over the semester: their pottery got better and better.

They were encouraged to put in as many reps as possible, regardless of the outcome. The result? Their reps turned into skills and turned into high quality pottery. At the end of the semester, they not only had the most pots, they had the best ones.

Moral of the story? Put in the reps.

My daily podcasting was my version of this. I piled up a lot of bad pots (episodes) over the first few months, but over time, my reps paid off. Yours will too.

* * *

To make mistakes is human. To own your mistakes is divine. Nothing elevates a person higher than quickly admitting and taking personal responsibility for the mistakes you make and then fixing them fairly. If you mess up, fess up. It's astounding how powerful this ownership is.

It's amazing how wonderful it feels to take 100 percent ownership of everything in your life. Most people spend so much time, energy, and mental bandwidth looking for people and situations to blame for their lousy lot in life. When you stop playing the blame game and take full ownership for exactly where you are in this world, everything changes.

You're a human being. You will screw up. Own it. Embrace it. Learn from it.

This attitude will keep you on the common path to uncommon success.

You got this!

*   *   *

You can obsess about serving your customers/audience/clients, or you can obsess about beating the competition. Both work, but of the two, obsessing about your customers will take you further.

Those on the common path to uncommon success choose a focus. Between your customers and competition, always focus on your customers. Learn from your competition, but obsess over your customers.

*   *   *

You are what you do. Not what you say, not what you believe, not how you vote, but what you spend your time on.

Take an honest assessment. How do you spend your days? Do you work out, eat healthy, drink water, and prioritize sleep? Then you are a very fit person.

Do you do the opposite? Then you are the opposite of a fit person.

How we spend our days is how we spend our lives, and how we spend our lives will be a direct reflection on the success (or lack thereof) we attain. We're on the path toward uncommon success. We spend our time on the right things that will allow us to achieve financial freedom and fulfillment.

You got this!

*   *   *

The universe is conspiring behind your back to make you a success. This will be much easier to do if you embrace this pronoia.

I had to google the definition of "pronoia." It is the opposite of paranoia. Specifically, the suspicion that the universe is conspiring on your behalf. Since you can choose your mindset, why not choose one of optimism? You're already stacking the odds in your favor by reading this book.

Embrace the reality that the stars are aligned for you to achieve uncommon success and carry that mentality with you in every endeavor you undertake.

You got this!

The Well of Knowledge, Naval Ravikant Edition

Naval is someone I was introduced to on *The Tim Ferriss Show*. I was instantly drawn to his concise, simple, and clear thoughts on life. I hope you are too.

You can find Naval on twitter @Naval.

* * *

Be a rational optimist.

You have two choices in life: be a pessimist or be an optimist. Of the two, an optimist will find the common path to uncommon success an easier and more enjoyable road.

Since you're going to choose to be an optimist, it might as well be a rational optimist. There's no need to waste time, energy, and bandwidth on irrational hopes, dreams, or ideas. We need to be lasered in our focus, rational with our goals, and patient with our results.

* * *

Avoid competition by being authentic.

So often, people see others having success in a certain area and launch a weak imitation and are surprised when their results are weak. The world is a competitive place. When you're on the path toward uncommon success, you can avoid getting crushed by the competition by simply being you: authentic, transparent, vulnerable you.

* * *

Treat everyone with respect.

I love the quote "Be nice to everyone on your way up so they'll be nice to you on your way down." Life is a roller coaster, and when you treat everyone with respect, they'll never forget. There will be a time you need a favor, or a friend, or a confidant. Those whom you treated with respect will be there for you. Also, it's the right thing to do, and when in doubt, do the right thing.

* * *

Be impatient with actions, patient with results.

If your default switch is action, your results will come. Remember my earlier example of the pottery class? Those who took imperfect action daily had the best results by the end of the experiment. You need to be like a horse at the starting gate every morning, ready to burst out of the blocks and start taking action. As for the results, be patient—they'll come.

* * *

He or she who experiments the most wins.

This is a perfect follow-up to the above. If Thomas Edison stopped experimenting after five thousand tries, he would have failed. Instead, he kept on experimenting, and after over ten thousand tries, he found success. Throw that pasta against the wall my friends, and never stop.

* * *

Inspiration has an expiration date.

Writing this book has been a passion project. I was *fired up* writing the first word and the sixty-thousandth word. However, I knew my best writing came first thing in the morning. It was when my inspiration was at its highest.

The first hour of every day for *months* was dedicated to writing this book. By 3:00 p.m., my inspiration for any project had expired. Moral of the story? When you find yourself with inspiration, *work*.

* * *

Play stupid games win stupid prizes.

I love this quote for its bluntness and truth. It's so easy to play stupid games in today's world. Buying followers on social media, overpromising while under-delivering, faking it till you make it.

These are all stupid games and you get stupid prizes. You'll never achieve financial freedom and fulfillment because you aren't delivering a true solution to a real problem. On the common path to uncommon success, we play the right games and win amazing prizes.

You got this!

* * *

Millionaires aren't busy, or productive, or the hardest and longest working people, they are those who produce the right things.

I can personally vouch for the above. My net worth is well into the eight figures and I am not busy. Most of my workdays are short and it's very rare I work hard for long stretches. Instead, I work hard in short, efficient sprints where I produce the *right* things. Are you producing the right things?

* * *

People have already dug in all of the obvious places, you have to be willing to dig deeper or in new areas.

This goes back to chapter 2: discover your niche. If you launch a weak imitation of a strong and entrenched competitor, you'll get crushed. If you're willing to dig deeper in new areas, identify problems that have not been sufficiently solved, you'll carve out a niche that will lead you to financial freedom and fulfillment.

Let's get digging!

* * *

Become top 25 percent at three things and combine them to become top 1 percent.

I think this is a great option for those who are struggling to discover their niche. What if you found three things that you can be the top 25 percent in, combined them, and became the top 1 percent within that combination? An example would be a Yoga instructor, who specifically served vegans who were also blind.

If you reached the top 25 percent in all three of those categories (which is very attainable), and combined them all, you would be in the top 1 percent of that combination. Get inventive, have fun, and *ignite!*

* * *

Future millionaires live at the edge of knowledge. Specific knowledge.

The key word here is *specific*. When I was a future millionaire, I was living on the edge of specific knowledge: how to create, grow, and monetize a daily interview podcast.

What is your specific knowledge? If you hesitated, you have some work to do. Commit to living at the edge of specific knowledge and staying there. It's fun!

* * *

As long as you are the best at it, the internet allows you to scale out.

This is once again showing just how powerful it is to discover your niche. If you are not the best in your niche, it's time to niche down again until you are the best. Sometimes being the best means being the only. Once you are the best, the internet will provide you leverage to grow a business that will allow you to achieve financial freedom and fulfillment.

Be the best.

* * *

You can become rich by giving people what they want at scale.

What are your avatar's biggest struggles, obstacles, and challenges? How can you provide the solution?

Once you've identified the delivery mechanism for the solution, the next project is discovering how to deliver that solution at scale. Delivering solutions at scale will result in uncommon success.

You got this!

* * *

A busy calendar and a busy mind will destroy your ability to do great things in this world.

Whenever people share how busy they are, I picture a car on blocks with the gas pedal jammed to the floor. The wheels are spinning, the engine is revving, but you're going nowhere. This is how 99 percent of the people in this world operate daily.

You're reading this book because you're looking to join the 1 percent of us who have achieved financial freedom and fulfillment. Those on the common path to uncommon success have clear calendars and clear minds. When we work, we work *hard* and we work on the *right* things. When we rest, we recover and let our minds and bodies refresh.

You got this!

I HOPE YOU enjoyed The Well of Knowledge. Remember, this well is meant to be revisited every time you feel thirsty for inspiration, motivation, and direction. The common path to uncommon success can be a long, hot, and dusty road. Slake your thirst here often, and financial freedom and fulfillment will be yours!

Check out your free companion course for added support along *The Common Path to Uncommon Success*: EOFire.com/success-course.

EPILOGUE

I'VE BEEN OPEN, HONEST, and transparent with you at every step of the common path to uncommon success. I'm not going to stop now.

Sometimes the truth hurts, but I'm sharing this truth out of love. If you're not currently enjoying financial freedom and fulfillment, you're coming up short on at least one step of the common path, possibly multiple.

I know what it takes to run a successful business for the long haul. It takes time, patience, persistence, and hard work. Uncommon success will not come overnight, but it will be yours if you commit to following the common path laid out in this book.

Every time you find yourself in need of motivation or inspiration, refer to The Well of Knowledge. It won't disappoint.

Every time you feel like something is not quite clicking in your business, refer to the table of contents. You should be able to identify an area you're neglecting or overlooking. Plug up that hole and you'll be back on track.

Remember, the world is ever evolving and so will your path to uncommon success. Once you've used this book to lay down the foundation, you'll be able to identify and exploit opportunities as they arise.

Trust the process, commit to the journey, and financial freedom and fulfillment will be yours.

—John Lee Dumas

INDEX

ABOUT THE AUTHOR

John Lee Dumas (JLD) is the founder and host of the award-winning podcast *Entrepreneurs on Fire*. Past guests include Tony Robbins, Barbara Corcoran, Seth Godin, and Gary Vaynerchuk. With more than 1 million monthly listens and more than 100 million total listens of his 3000+ episodes, JLD is spreading entrepreneurial FIRE on a global scale.

Getting his entrepreneurial start back in 2012, JLD identified the need for a daily podcast sharing inspiration, motivation, and business lessons from the world's top entrepreneurs. Following Gandhi's advice to "be the change you wish to see in the world," JLD set out to make his dream a reality.

With zero audience and no prior broadcasting experience, JLD launched *Entrepreneurs On Fire* in September 2012.

By the end of 2013, JLD had built *Entrepreneurs On Fire* into a media empire that was generating more than $100,000 in net profit every month. That same year, he launched Podcasters' Paradise, which is now the largest subscription-based online podcasting community in the world, teaching others how to create, grow, and monetize their own podcasts.

In 2016, JLD published his first of three physical journals, *The Freedom Journal: Accomplish Your #1 Goal in 100 Days*, which generated $453,000 in its first thirty days. In 2017, he published *The Mastery Journal: Master Productivity, Discipline, and Focus in 100 Days* and generated more than $280,000 in the first thirty days. And in 2018, he launched *The Podcast Journal: Idea to Launch in 50 Days*, which is a top-selling podcast journal on Amazon. Combined, he's sold more than a hundred thousand copies and impacted millions through his podcast, online courses, communities, masterminds, and journals. You can learn more at EOFire.com.

The Common Path to Uncommon Success is his first traditionally published book, which he hopes will launch the careers of millions of aspiring entrepreneurs in the years to come.